I0042826

THE MARKETING OF DEBT

THE MARKETING OF DEBT

How They Get You

BY

JOHN B. DINSMORE

Wright State University, USA

emerald
PUBLISHING

United Kingdom – North America – Japan
India – Malaysia – China

Emerald Publishing Limited
Emerald Publishing, Floor 5, Northspring, 21-23 Wellington Street, Leeds
LS1 4DL

First edition 2025

Copyright © 2025 John B. Dinsmore.
Published under exclusive licence by Emerald Publishing Limited.

Reprints and permissions service
Contact: www.copyright.com

No part of this book may be reproduced, stored in a retrieval
system, transmitted in any form or by any means electronic,
mechanical, photocopying, recording or otherwise without either
the prior written permission of the publisher or a licence permitting
restricted copying issued in the UK by The Copyright Licensing
Agency and in the USA by The Copyright Clearance Center. Any
opinions expressed in the chapters are those of the authors. Whilst
Emerald makes every effort to ensure the quality and accuracy of its
content, Emerald makes no representation implied or otherwise, as
to the chapters' suitability and application and disclaims any
warranties, express or implied, to their use.

British Library Cataloguing in Publication Data
A catalogue record for this book is available from the British Library

ISBN: 978-1-83662-601-5 (Print)
ISBN: 978-1-83662-598-8 (Online)
ISBN: 978-1-83662-600-8 (Epub)

INVESTOR IN PEOPLE

This book is dedicated to the memory of Steve Guerrier, Professor of History at James Madison University.

I am a drummer. And what made me want to become a drummer was listening to, and watching, John Bonham of Led Zeppelin. It wasn't just his formidable skill. It was his joy in doing it. And, though I was pretty sure I wouldn't be able to play as well as him, I wanted to feel that feeling, or at least something close to it.

The first time I took a history class with Steve Guerrier was a similar experience. His mastery of the topic and spellbinding storytelling lured me in. But, it was his joy in doing it, his strong connection to those around him, and the sense that he was – without a doubt – where he was supposed to be, doing what he was supposed to be doing, that made me think, "If I could do something like that…"

John Bonham's son became a drummer. Steve Guerrier's daughter became a historian. But, of course. When you have a front row seat to inspired performance, you seek out inspiration for yourself. It makes you want to take the stage.

I'll never be able to play drums like John Bonham nor will I ever be able to teach as well as Steve Guerrier. But I do know their joy. And I'm pretty sure I've helped others find that same joy.

For that, I am eternally grateful.

CONTENTS

FOREWORD: THE TRUE PURPOSE OF MARKETING

Jason Harris
Cofounder, CEO, Mekanism

Best-selling author of *The Soulful Art of Persuasion*

"Oh, that's just marketing."

We've all heard that dismissive phrase equating marketing with manipulation, empty promises, and glossy distractions. As someone who has dedicated his career to advertising, I understand the skepticism. Marketing consistently ranks shoulder-to-shoulder among the least trusted industries with its cousin, advertising. According to a recent Gallup Poll, the three least trusted professions are: car salespersons, congress people, and advertising practitioners. I have always taken offense to this characterization. So when people say "that's just marketing," what they're really saying is: "That's just smoke and mirrors designed to separate you from your money."

But here's the truth: This widespread cynicism about marketing doesn't stem from what marketing is – it stems from what it has become in the hands of those who abuse it.

Think about your worst experiences as a customer. Perhaps it was that "unlimited" plan with hidden limits buried in fine print. Or that "revolutionary" product that revolutionized nothing but your bank balance. Or that "APR increase" that was printed in mouse type that you could never even read if you tried. These hit-and-run transactions leave us feeling victimized, our trust betrayed, our wallets lighter. Research shows that these negative experiences stick with us, disproportionately influencing our future purchasing decisions. Once burned, twice shy.

But what if I told you that real marketing – true marketing – is actually about creating harmony between what organizations can offer and what people genuinely need?

Harvard economist Michael Porter defines marketing as the art of creating fit between an organization and the outside world. At its core, marketing is about.

- Creating products that solve real problems.

- Making these solutions easily accessible.

- Pricing them fairly and clearly.

- Communicating their benefits honestly.

When marketing is done right, it creates a virtuous cycle. Customers find products that genuinely improve their lives. Companies build sustainable growth through repeat business rather than one-time transactions.

Look at the brands you truly love – the ones whose logos you proudly wear, whose products you enthusiastically recommend to friends. These companies aren't just selling products; they're creating relationships. They've earned your trust not through slick advertising campaigns and hidden fees but through consistent delivery of real value. They don't see you as just a wallet to be emptied.

Ethical marketing doesn't hide the risks; it helps consumers make informed decisions. It trusts that an educated customer is the best customer.

Authentic marketing stands out like a lighthouse in the fog in a world drowning in hucksterism and hollow promises. When companies demonstrate genuine empathy and understanding – when they pull back from the aggressive "always be closing" mindset and instead focus on "always be helping" – they don't just find customers. They build a long-term community.

This book is about highlighting the egregious techniques that some industries use. And it is about rediscovering marketing's true purpose: creating meaningful connections between organizations and the people they serve. It's about building businesses that don't just survive through clever tactics but thrive through genuine value creation.

In the end, the best marketing isn't about separating people from their money – it's about connecting people with solutions, products, and services they want and need.

ACKNOWLEDGMENTS

Writing a book is a massive undertaking full of manic moments of inspiration, self-doubt, stress, and satisfaction. There are a great many people who have helped me through the process, tolerated my ranting and procrastination, and encouraged me along the way.

First and foremost, my wife Elissa, who helped me change careers when it didn't really make sense on any level. She gave up her job, moved to a place that was not a top-10 destination for her, and worked to put me through school. All just so she didn't have to see a defeated look on my face in the morning before I headed off to job I didn't like. Twenty years in and it's still a good time. I love you.

To my boys Johnny and Owen. You amaze me, amuse me, and teach me on a daily basis.

My colleagues at Wright State University – you've made this the best job I've ever had. To Mike Urick for being a good friend and introducing me to Fiona at Emerald who agreed to publish my book. To Fiona, Yemaya, and everyone at Emerald, thanks for taking a chance on me and helping me figure out what I was doing. For a while there, it looked like I was creating 200 pages of kindling and you provided much needed guidance.

To Mom, Dad, Jim, Ellen, Hank, Liz, Mike, Ally, Minnow, Rocco, and Michael, you mean more to me than you'll ever know. To Jason Harris... from writing the foreword of this book to letting my band practice in your basement in college, you've always said yes to me, and I'm not really sure why. Thank you. Watching your success has been a lot of fun, and it couldn't have happened to a nicer guy.

1

TRIPPING THE DEBT TRAP

The dangers of debt are hardly a secret. Yet, most of us fall into the debt trap at some point. Why? We *think* we understand how debt works. Research shows that almost none of us actually do.

That's a dangerous proposition. All of us will take on multiple forms of debt over the course of our adult lives. How we navigate these financial instruments will have a dramatic impact on the success, relationships, happiness, and even health of ourselves and those we love.

Why do we have such a hard time understanding debt? The truth is that we are psychologically predisposed to *mis*understanding it. All of us have biases, blind spots, and confused rationalizations that act as gremlins sabotaging the management of our personal finances. Those gremlins encourage us to underestimate the costs of debt and overestimate our ability to pay.

Marketers not only know this but embrace it. They use it to their advantage by promoting debt in a way that distracts us from understanding the risks of what they're selling. In other words, the financial industry not only sets the gremlins free but also gives them each an espresso and a massive dose of steroids.

Imagine if, despite most adults owning cars, almost nobody understood how to drive one. There would be mass carnage on the highway. Now imagine if the automobile industry was actively attempting to misinform the public about how to operate a vehicle, thinking that more crashes would help drive sales of new cars.

Madness. This is analogous to what is happening in financial services.

The good news is that:

- The automobile industry does not encourage the incompetent operation of its products;

- Society requires aspiring drivers to pass skills and knowledge tests before getting behind the wheel.

These things help protect not only the driver but also the general public. But no such precautions exist for personal finance. Despite the high stakes of managing debt, anyone with a pen and a pulse can apply for a loan – regardless if they understand what they're doing. And some in the financial services industry are actively attempting to distract and misinform their customers to boost the bottom line. It's a disaster for the borrower and society as a whole.

Chances are, you've struggled with debt at one point or another. Most of us have. For whatever reason. Maybe our eyes got bigger than our incomes when it came to making a purchase. Or maybe we just had a run of bad luck.

Whatever the case, getting in over your head with debt is an experience that is as universal as it is unpleasant. The anxiety. The self-doubt. The helplessness. Plus, clawing yourself out of debt – and staying out of it – requires constant vigilance and intense self-discipline. Even then, it may still not be enough.

This book looks at the struggles we all have in making decisions about debt and the psychology behind why we struggle. Then, we'll examine common marketing tactics that exploit our cognitive blind spots and trick us into getting deeper in debt. Lastly, we'll examine how we can make better financial decisions going forward.

WHY IS FINANCIAL DECISION-MAKING SO DIFFICULT?

The economist Herbert Simon coined the term "bounded rationality" about humans.[1] It's a term that always makes me laugh. Why?

---

[1]Simon, H. A. (1957). *Models of man; social and rational.* Wiley.

Because, despite the clinical sound of the term, its inherent meaning is that every person is at least a little dumb and/or crazy sometimes. Actually, most of the time. This means me. And it means you, too. (Sorry.)

Bounded rationality means that we have limits to our judgment and decision-making. We run into those limitations for a myriad of reasons: too much information, too little information, over-stimulation, fatigue, biases, moods, and so on. With all these limitations, it's kind of amazing that we ever make good decisions at all.

The reason why it's hard to make good decisions is that decision-making is not just about the intelligence of a person. If it were, then all of our lives – and the world in general – would be much better off. The world would be built on a foundation of mostly solid decision-making. But, it's not.

There is some amount of luck involved in making a good decision. The "luck" element means that, at the point of decision-making, the decision-maker, the information provided/available, and the decision-making environment are all in an optimal state. And that rarely happens.

There's too much to know, not enough time to learn it, too many decisions to make, and a gazillion other factors impacting our cognitive and emotional states. Maybe you didn't get enough sleep last night. Or perhaps you have incomplete information. Or maybe still, you have the right information and are in a good state of mind, but your neighbor's 22 rottweilers are barking their heads off and you just can't process with all that noise. Any of these scenarios are enough to derail your judgment and decision-making.

In the gap between what we should know in order to make a decision, and what we have the wherewithal (time, energy) to understand, we make decisions of varying quality. That, unfortunately, is life. And as a result, we all have decisions for which we'd like do-overs.

We sign up to have vegan meal kits mailed to our homes even though the only thing we hate more than cooking is eating vegetables. The infomercial persuades you to buy The Abdominizer™ even though you'd rather have your teeth pulled than do a sit-up. You agree to pay $1,000 for undercarriage treatment on a new car despite not being sure what an undercarriage is or how (or for what) it's being treated. It happens to all of us. We all make these silly, irrational, embarrassing, and sometimes expensive or otherwise harmful decisions. No doubt, even Albert Einstein periodically smacked himself in the forehead and thought "I'm such an idiot!" after buying something he didn't really want or need.

The good news is that these goofy decisions aren't a reflection of your intelligence (at least, not usually). The bad news is you're likely to do it again. Repeatedly. But where marketers can make matters worse is when they exploit our cognitive shortcomings to produce a harmful, ruinous, or even deadly, outcome.

Many of the products we consume are vital to modern life: consumer credit, pharmaceuticals, and others. Other products or services, such as gambling or alcohol, are harmless amusements if done in moderation. But all these products have negative consequences – often severe – if misused. And the more marketers do to decrease consumers' understanding about the inherent risks of these products, the more likely consumers are to misuse them.

That's where this book comes in. This is your guide to understanding our natural limitations in judgment and decision-making and how marketers of debt take advantage of those limits. And, with that understanding, it should help you make better financial decisions.

A PRIMER ON READING ABOUT BEHAVIORAL RESEARCH

This book extensively cites and discusses leading peer-reviewed research on human behavior. This is not to be confused with many of the behavioral anecdotes or slogans you see in clickbait and social media. Too often we see pseudo-psychology, easy answers, and motivational mantras getting mainstream acceptance, despite their having never actually been tested. "Become rich…a better parent and/ or spouse…smarter…taller…more attractive…with these three easy steps." And, in reality, these things are either based on one person's intuition or an author or publisher's instinct that it's something people will buy. After all, easy solutions are a lot more marketable than difficult ones.

When you hear someone offering easy solutions to difficult problems, do yourself a favor: change the channel, unfollow the account, and, above all, hold on to your wallet. That person is selling a fantasy. Changing your behavior or improving your decision-making is *hard* – always has been, always will be.

If it were easy, we'd all have six-pack abs and no family awkwardness at Thanksgiving. But, alas dear reader, we know that's not the case. Thanksgiving seems to get more awkward every year and our abs, well, the less said about those, the better. And nobody's "three easy steps" are going to change that. Sometimes you just have to eat your vegetables.

Consider this book your broccoli. And where possible, I will slather the broccoli in gooey nacho cheese to make it go down easier. We will review some of the major theories and research from psychology, economics, and marketing about our vulnerabilities in assessing debt and tie it to the marketing of loans. And, if I do my job, you'll learn a few things you didn't know before and maybe avoid making a regrettable financial decision down the road. That would be sweet.

Understand that this book avoids going down rabbit holes or doing any of the navel-gazing you associate with academia. Instead, we will discuss – in real terms – how behavioral research *often* explains our poor judgment and decision-making on debt. Then, we will look at how the marketing of debt exploits those mental blind spots and gets us deeper in hock.

At the same time, this book will avoid painting with too broad a brush. You will notice the use of qualifiers like "often," "usually," "in general," or "typically." You will also notice the words "always" or "never" are not used. Here's why: people and situations are different and complex. If you look at some of the most prominent and tested behavioral science out there, you will find that there are exceptions. Certain types of people behave one way in a situation, while other types of people behave differently.

Here's an example: later in this book, we will discuss something called "loss aversion," also known as Prospect Theory. This is a theory that has garnered its creators, Daniel Kahneman and Amos Tversky, a Nobel Prize and many other accolades. Even theories that are offshoots of Prospect Theory, like Mental Accounting, have won Nobel Prizes.

Kahneman and Tversky are so prominent that Michael Lewis, renowned author of *The Big Short, The Blind Side*, and *Moneyball*, wrote a bestselling book about them called *The Undoing Project*. Looking at Google Scholar, the works of *either* Daniel Kahneman or Amos Tversky individually have been cited more than the works of Stephen Hawking and Albert Einstein *combined*. So, Prospect Theory is a big deal. And its authors are rightfully considered among the best to have ever conducted behavioral research.

Yet, a series of studies was published a few years ago saying Prospect Theory was, if you'll pardon my scientific jargon, a bunch of nonsense.[2] A little while after that, another series of studies was published saying that the "bunch of nonsense" paper was, in fact, a bunch of nonsense.[3]

More specifically, the latter paper found that Prospect Theory *is* valid, but it affects people differently depending on the individual and context. And that is the case with nearly every psychological or economic theory. People – and the situations they find themselves in – are unique. The pursuit of universal truths to human behavior is a fool's errand.

Such a scenario is not uncommon in science. The popular [mis] conception of scientific research is that a single discovery in a lab somewhere produces an unassailable truth. But the reality is that any scientific discovery is the beginning of the process, not the end. Each newly identified phenomenon will have drivers, amplifiers, and exceptions that vary according to a wide variety of factors. Isaac Newton developed a theory of gravity saying that what goes up must come down.[4] Centuries later, Orville and Wilbur Wright found/invented an exception.

This may cause you to wonder: If there are no universal truths, why should I read this book? The answer is that this book ties

---

[2]Gal, D., & Rucker, D. D. (2018). The loss of loss aversion: Will it loom larger than its gain? *Journal of Consumer Psychology, 28*(3), 497–516.
[3]Mrkva, K., Johnson, E. J., Gächter, S., & Herrmann, A. (2020). Moderating loss aversion: Loss aversion has moderators, but reports of its death are greatly exaggerated. *Journal of Consumer Psychology, 30*(3), 407–428.
[4]Yes, physicists, I understand this is a massive oversimplification.

common (though – again – not universal) debt-related mistakes that people make to scientific research explaining why they make them. Some things you read about may make you think, "That's not me." Great! Enjoy reading about the rest of us poor suckers who *are* like that.

But some other things will ring true and make you think, "OMG, I *totally* do that," or "I know someone who does that." And, if that's the case, you might pick up on some things that could help you make better choices. And, again, that would be sweet.

2

A SOCIETY DROWNING IN DEBT

Financial services such as banking, credit cards, and mortgages are essential to living in modern society. They enable a wide array of societal goods such as buying homes, advancing educations, providing for retirement, and more. But with all the good they do, there are clearly excesses.

In 2021, Americans had about $15 trillion in consumer debt, $10.76 trillion in housing debt (mortgages and home equity lines of credit), and $4.19 trillion in other consumer debt (credit cards, car loans, student loans, etc.).[1] Per US Household, that works out to roughly $88,000 in housing debt and $34,000 in non-housing debt.

Those are BIG numbers – so big, in fact, that it's hard to get a real sense of what they mean. The United States is too big and too diverse in terms of cost of living, income, and home ownership to make such numbers more than an abstraction. So, let's look at just credit card debt by income in the United States (Table 1).[2]

If you've ever had to pay down credit cards (and most of us have)... it's hard! Many people run up credit card debt because their incomes weren't meeting expenses in the first place. Now, to pay it down, you have to come up with money to cover your basic

---

[1]New York Federal Reserve Bank. (n.d.). Household debt and credit report, Q2 2021. https://www.newyorkfed.org/microeconomics/hhdc.html. Accessed on September 16, 2021.
[2]Fay, B. (2021, May 6). Demographics of debt. https://www.debt.org/faqs/americans-in-debt/demographics/. Accessed on September 16, 2021.

Table 1. Levels of Credit Card Debt by Income in the United States.

Income	Avg. Credit Card Debt	Debt as Pct of Income
$290,000 or more	$12,600	4.34% or less
$152,000 to $290,999	$9,780	4.42%
$95,00 to $151,999	$6,990	5.66%
$59,000 to $94,999	$4,910	6.38%
$35,000 to $58,999	$4,650	9.89%
$34,999 or less	$3,830	10.94% or more

Source: 2021 Value Penguin analysis of census and Federal Reserve reports.

expenses – which you didn't have – and then earn *more* to pay it down. Plus, when you consider that the poorer you are:

- the less money you have;

- the more you have to pay for your debt in terms of interest rate;

- the more you pay for basic common goods and services such as groceries.[3]

That is a particularly tough place to be.

And there are *so many* types of debt out there! Home mortgages, mortgage refinance loans, business loans, construction loans, payday loans, car loans, car title loans, student loans, credit cards, home equity lines of credit, and on and on. And after you have availed yourself of all these different types of debt products, you will no doubt need a debt consolidation loan. And if you do this a few times over, you might even need a loan to consolidate your debt consolidation loans. (Yes, really.)

---

[3]Weese, K. Why it costs so much to be poor in America. *Washington Post.* https://www.washingtonpost.com/news/posteverything/wp/2018/01/25/why-it-costs-so-much-to-be-poor-in-america/. Accessed on September 16, 2021.

WELL-INTENTIONED FINANCIAL PRODUCTS

As mentioned, there are a great variety of loans out there. Many are well-intentioned and produce vital benefits to individuals and society as a whole. These include traditional mortgages, Veteran's Administration loans, student loans, small business loans, and auto loans. They stimulate the economy, enable home ownership, and create business and educational opportunities. These financial products have market-rate (or below) levels of interest and are intended as catalysts to wealth creation through home ownership, college education, entrepreneurship, and more.

Yes, banks still make money off these. And, yes, many of these loans can come in less benevolent, higher interest forms. But, for the most part, these are loans that create businesses, jobs, and wealth. They enable personal and professional fulfillment. And they do so at a reasonable cost.

Plus, products like Veteran's Administration loans can provide these benefits to groups who are often less affluent – and therefore less likely to be extended credit – but who society values highly. These are all things that make our world a better place.

Despite the benevolent intent and structure of these loans, there are still ample opportunities to get into trouble. People can make bad borrowing or investment decisions. Or they can just be unlucky. Maybe the house they buy with their mortgage has a nuclear waste site go in next door. Or maybe their business partner takes all the proceeds from the commercial loan and runs away to Belize. Ouch.

Or ... maybe they borrow too much. And no matter how well-intentioned the loan, it *will* maul you if you're not careful. As an example, let's look at student loans.

Student loans provide opportunities for individuals to invest in themselves and their futures. Education, after all, is still the best predictor of income – and even lifespan – there is.[4] But people still get into plenty of trouble with these. Over the 2010s, the amount of student

---

[4]Lutz, W., & Kebede, E. (2018). Education and health: Redrawing the Preston curve. *Population and Development Review*, 44(2), 343.

debt in the United States doubled.[5] There are a lot of reasons for this, including[6]:

- rising tuition;

- rising cost of living;

- university administrators building unnecessary buildings to enhance their resumes;

- state governments reducing financial support/subsidies of public universities;

- universities using recruiting firms to boost enrollment that give almost half of tuition dollars to those firms;

- alleged price fixing at some colleges;[7]

- lack of controls on individual student loan borrowing;

- parents and kids making college selections based on the quality of the sushi in the cafeteria and/or the quality of the school's workout facilities;

- lack of risk to student lenders (student loans – unlike virtually every other form of debt – cannot be discharged in bankruptcy);

- bad actors in higher-ed such as certain for-profit colleges whose entire revenue model is built on getting prospective students over-leveraged on student loans regardless of their ability to afford payments or complete their degree.

But the fact remains that a college degree is the price of admission to most careers. And with that cost having increased 140% (after adjustments for inflation) over what it used to, it's no wonder that

---

[5]Hess, A. US student debt has more than doubled over the last 10 years. *CNBC.com.* https://www.cnbc.com/2020/12/22/us-student-debt-has-increased-by-more-than-100percent-over-past-10-years.html. Accessed on February 11, 2022.
[6]Oh, don't get me started on the many unnecessary costs associated with higher education. OK, well, I'll get a little started here.
[7]Saul, S., & Hartecollis, A. (2022, February 21). Lawsuit says 16 elite colleges are part of price fixing cartel. *The New York Times.* https://www.nytimes.com/2022/01/10/us/financial-aid-lawsuit-colleges.html

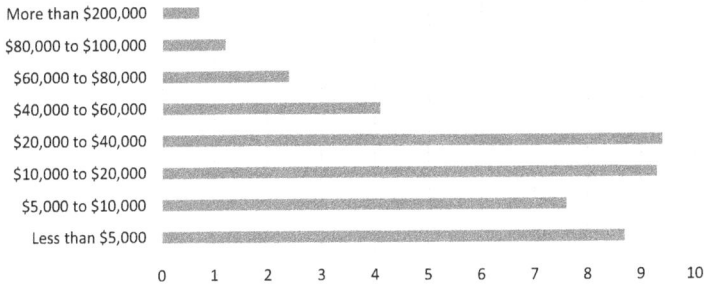

Fig. 1. Number of Student Loan Borrowers by Amount Borrowed (in Millions).

69% of all college students take out these loans (Fig. 1).[8,9] What choice do they have?

Student loans are perhaps the most benevolent of loans. They were created to bring opportunity to those who might otherwise not be able to afford it. But, if misused or misunderstood, they can take on quite a different appearance.

These are debt products that exist to achieve self-fulfillment and perhaps even yield a return in the form of enhanced earnings. And yet, as you can see from these exhibits, it's still very easy to get into some major trouble with these more traditional – and well-intentioned – loans.

ZOMBIE LOANS

Then, on the other end of the debt spectrum, we have what we'll call zombie loans. These are products such as payday loans, car title loans, and pawn shops. Zombie loans target primarily the poor and financially inexperienced with exorbitant interest rates that leave them in a far worse place when all is said and done. And like with any zombie movie, once a borrower touches a zombie loan,

---

[8]Bouchrika, I. How much has college tuition increased in the last 10 years? *Research.com*. https://research.com/universities-colleges/college-tuition-increase. Accessed on February 11, 2022.
[9]A look at the shocking student loan debt statistics for 2022. *StudentLoanHero.com*. https://studentloanhero.com/student-loan-debt-statistics/. Accessed on February 11, 2022.

the overwhelming likelihood is it drains the borrower of any financial life.

You do not stand a chance against a zombie loan. Once a zombie loan like a car title loan has you in its grips, it's at least taking a chunk out of you. And with interest rates sometime exceeding 300% (not a typo), an encounter with a single zombie loan dramatically increases the likelihood of future zombie encounters.

Let's look at car title loans, probably the least known of the zombie loans but one of the most vicious. Here's how they work. Having trouble making rent? Give me the title to your $4,000 car in exchange for this $400 loan, and if you can't pay me $700 in a few weeks, the car is mine. A rotten deal, to be sure. But if you're desperate enough (and who's not desperate to keep a roof over their head?) it can seem the only solution to people under significant stress.

Car title loans are so egregious, a number of states (but not all!) have passed laws saying you can't charge people more than 300% interest on a loan. And unconscionable interest rates are just one aspect of zombie loans. Loans targeting the poor are often riddled with booby traps that include[10]:

- *Hidden fees:* Charges to the borrower that aren't called "interest" but still go into the lender's pocket.

- *Prepayment penalties:* If you would like to pay off your loan ahead of time, it's going to cost you extra, just so the lender can still get the interest.

- *Balloon payments:* Smaller payments at the beginning of the loan that make it seem more affordable before escalating to a less affordable monthly payment.

These are all mechanisms that make sure the lender gets its [exorbitant] interest regardless of how responsibly the borrower behaves. And, these traps enable the lender to advertise "low monthly

[10]Fay, B. What is predatory lending? *Debt.org.* https://www.debt.org/credit/predatory-lending/. Accessed on February 21, 2022.

payments" and "low interest" when, in fact, the interest is being called something else or the high interest payments are merely being delayed a bit.

The Inherent Pitfalls of Financial Decision-Making

Whatever loan you're dealing with, all of these products require the borrower to make certain judgments:

- Estimating your future ability to pay.

- Trading off one goal for another.

- Making some attempt at math.

- Understanding the true cost of a loan.

- Being able to treat all income and expenses in a rational and consistent manner.

As mentioned in the first chapter, humans are limited in their cognitive abilities. There's only so much brain to go around. And every choice and decision we have to make during the day reduces our available cognitive resources. This is especially the case given the vast number of decisions and other mental tasks (like remembering where we put our car keys) each of us must complete every single day.

When you combine that with the nature of financial decision-making and marketers potentially obscuring some of a debt product's more vicious features... These aren't the types of decisions that play to our intellectual strengths. In fact, it's a minefield of biases, blind spots, and confusion.

In the coming chapters, we'll look at each of these aspects of financial decision-making, the research on why we struggle with them, how certain marketing tactics exploit our limitations, and what we can do about it.

3

THE ABSTRACT FUTURE

Core to any decision about using credit is some estimation of your future circumstances. Whether it's credit cards, student loans, mortgages, or some other debt instrument, the borrower has to look at how much payments on that loan will be and for how long. Then, the borrower has to determine if he/she will be able to meet that obligation over time.

It is a series of actions that preys on some of the most glaring weaknesses of human judgment. In fact, research consistently shows that humans are *terrible* at estimating their future circumstances.[1] We consistently err on the side of being overly optimistic about what the future holds for us.

SCOTT'S TOTS

In an episode of the American version of the TV hit *The Office* entitled "Scott's Tots," bumbling boss Michael Scott is called to meet with a group of graduating high school seniors.[2] Ten years prior, he had

---

[1]Soman, D., & Cheema, A. (2002). The effect of credit on spending decisions: The role of the credit limit and credibility. *Marketing Science*, *21*(1), 32–53.
[2]Stupnitsky, G. (Writer), Eisenberg, L. (Writer), Novak, B. J. (Director). (2009, December 3). Scott's tots [Season 6, Episode 12]. In *The Office*. Deedle Dee Productions.

spoken to these same kids as third graders and promised to pay the entire class' way through college.

The episode is based on the real-life story of Eugene Lang, a wealthy investor who promised a sixth-grade class in Harlem that he would pay for their college. Mr. Lang not only kept that promise but he sent about 16,000 more students through college in his remaining years.

The loveable but foolish Michael Scott had good intentions similar to Mr. Lang but... no such resources. Now that he was being called upon to live up to his promise, he had to confess he didn't have the money to put one kid through college, let alone an entire graduating class, saying:

> *I'm not a millionaire. I thought I would be by the time I was thirty. . . but I wasn't even close. Then I thought maybe I would be by the time I was forty. . . but by forty I had less money than when I was thirty. Maybe by my fifties. . . I don't know.*

If you've seen the episode, you had a good time laughing at Mr. Scott. But the truth is, his behavior is very human and relatable. *Most of us*, to some degree, have been guilty of this same thing: over-estimating our future circumstances. We are sure that, in the future, our new ventures will succeed brilliantly, the big promotion will come through, and that our proverbial ship will come in. Never mind that our past and present have consistently told us life consists of both good fortune and bad and you can never be sure which awaits.

A more serious example comes from a documentary on D-Day about US forces landing at Normandy, France in World War II. They interviewed a man recounting his experience. He and his brothers in arms were briefed by their commanding officer about the perilous mission ahead. The commanding officer said that, in all likelihood, two-thirds of them would not survive. The soldier, then 18 years old, recalled looking to the men on either side of him and thinking, "Those poor bastards." Rather than thinking he had a 66% chance of killed, he immediately thought the two guys next to him had 100% chance of not making it through and that he would be fine.

We are, as a species, optimistic and hopeful about our future being brighter than our present – despite the fact that things can, and sometimes do, get worse. Life is, after all, messy and unpredictable.

And the younger we are, not only the more optimistic we tend to be but the more likely we are to be encountering debt for the first time.[3] This spells trouble as naivete and debt are a bad combination.

Earliest forms of debt we encounter are usually in the form of student loans or our first credit cards. Ambitious 17–18 year-olds are being asked to take on increasing amounts of student loan debt in hopes getting a college degree and being competitive in the job market.[4] In the process, they are also being asked to commit to a major and career path in which they have no idea they will either flourish or enjoy. It doesn't really make sense.

Predicting the future is problematic. It's also an exercise that's often unnecessarily expensive. Why?

THE PSYCHOLOGY OF THE FUTURE

In a sense, the optimism we have about the future is the ultimate survival resource for human beings: the belief that no matter how bad things are now, they will get better. It would be pretty hard to get out of bed if we believed otherwise. It would be almost impossible for that soldier on D-Day to board the landing vessel if he thought his demise was certain.

Optimism is a bias. It affects our judgment and decision-making without our realizing it. And, like any other bias, optimism causes us to not see the world how it is, but in a way that conforms to our pre-conceived notions. While the optimism bias helps us to "keep on keeping on," it also can land us in hot water. Inherent in our optimism is the underestimation or misunderstanding of all kinds of risk – physical, financial, and otherwise. To take on bigger risks than you realize means to gamble more than you know. And, eventually, the probabilities win. You lose.

One of the places we are most optimistic about the future is in terms of how much money we think we'll have. In general, we think

---

[3]Klaczynski, P. A. (2017). Age differences in optimism bias are mediated by reliance on intuition and religiosity. *Journal of Experimental Child Psychology, 163*, 126–139.

[4]Gravely, A. (2021, November 16). Student debt from private lenders hits all-time high. *Inside Higher Ed.* https://www.insidehighered.com/news/2021/11/17/report-outlines-class-2020s-student-debt-burden

that all of the problems and constraints (time, money, energy) we face now will be worked out down the road. In our minds, the future is different, somehow. And because it seems or feels different, we treat decisions and judgments about the future differently. We even use different decision-making processes when considering future events versus those in the present.[5]

In economics, this principle is called *intertemporal discounting* – we value things in the future much differently than we do in the present. Not only do we value things differently between present and future but we value things differently depending on how far into the future they are. How much differently?

Let's look at some of the research on what makes us value the same thing very differently depending on whether that thing is happening today, in a few weeks, or 10 years from now. And then, lets look at how those differences cause us to make bone-headed financial decisions.

CUTTING YOURSELF SLACK

While economists have long examined intertemporal discounting, a couple of marketing professors (Gal Zauberman at Yale University and John Lynch at University of Colorado at Boulder) have further developed this into the concept of "resource slack."[6] This principle, at its most simple, states that people think they'll have more resources in the future than they have today. This, despite our years of experience clearly demonstrating that we won't!

Since we don't seem capable of learning this lesson, our lives become an endless loop of future commitments we make happily, but begin to dread as the time to fulfill those commitments draws near.

We easily commit time, money, and energy to future events. When we are later confronted with making good on these com-mitments, we are often filled with regret. Or, put differently, we

---

[5]Ersner-Hershfield, H., Wimmer, G. E., & Knutson, B. (2009). Saving for the future self: Neural measures of future self-continuity predict temporal discounting. *Social Cognitive and Affective Neuroscience, 4*(1), 85–92.
[6]Zauberman, G., & Lynch Jr., J. G. (2005). Resource slack and propensity to discount delayed investments of time versus money. *Journal of Experimental Psychology: General, 134*(1), 23.

agree to things in the future that we would never agree to in the present. In the present, we are acutely aware of our limitations – we're tired, pressed for time, and short on cash.

In the future, what limitations could we possibly have? The future is a place consisting only of free time and disposable income where we work-out constantly and start and maybe even complete home improvement projects. But this weekend? It's a crush of car pools, kids' soccer games, and maybe (doubtfully) – if there's time – getting to the grocery store. But a few weekends from now? Why, it's a veritable Utopia of inexhaustible time, money, and energy.

Sound ridiculous? It is! But that doesn't mean we don't do it.

Think about a good friend asking you for help moving – today. As you don't have other plans, you, as a dutiful friend, *might* head over at a moment's notice to start moving boxes. Or, more likely, you'll be exhausted and/or staring at a sink full of dirty dishes, or a lawn that needs to be mowed and say, "I just can't."

Now, if that friend asks you two weeks in advance? You'll likely commit with little reservation (other than the usual dread that moving brings). This, despite the fact you're almost always tired and behind on housework. And you most certainly will be on that moving day in two weeks. Instead, you think, "Eh, it probably won't be so bad." This is moving we're talking about. It *will* be that bad. In fact, it will be worse.

But, it's OK. We all do it.

We'll look at how this translates to financial decision-making in a moment. But first, if resource slack – underestimating the sacrifice and difficulty that future expenditures of time, money and energy represent – is *what* we do. Then, *why* do we do it? Why, despite a myriad of experiences that should have taught us better, do we keep repeating this mistake instead of – ya know – getting a clue?

PEOPLE DON'T UNDERSTAND THEIR EXPENSES

Most people don't understand their monthly expenses *today*, much less in the future. There is an error that people consistently make when it comes to estimating their future expenses known as "expense prediction bias."[7] The reason for this is that, as people attempt to estimate their expenses, they remember their regular expenses, but fail to recall their irregular ones.[8]

Irregular expenses are those that don't re-occur at a similar amount or regular time interval. Mortgage and utilities? Sure, you remember those. They happen at the same time every month in the same amounts. But repairs to your car or home? They happen at random intervals and have a very broad range of costs. We typically fail to take those frequent and common (but irregular and significant) expenses into account.

When you think about it, there are a large number of expenses that meet this description: car repairs, home repairs, taxes, tolls, parking, medical bills, clothing, entertainment, travel, and so on. They are "irregular" in the sense that they are not completely predictable in terms of amount and frequency. Yet, we have many "irregular" expenses every month.

So, people don't just underestimate their expenses by a few dollars, they do it on a massive scale. And this expense prediction bias acts as one of the more destructive gremlins in your mind when attempting to estimate your ability to meet a loan payment in the future.

HOW MARKETERS TAKE ADVANTAGE

If we:

- Think we'll have more money in the future than we are actually likely to have.

- Believe we have fewer expenses than we actually do...

It's not hard to see how many of us could be predisposed to taking on more debt that we can afford. But that's on us. Or, at least,

---

[7]Ülkümen, G., Thomas, M., & Morwitz, V. G. (2008). Will I spend more in 12 months or a year? The effect of ease of estimation and confidence on budget estimates. *Journal of Consumer Research*, 35(2), 245–256.
[8]Howard, R. C. C., Hardisty, D. J., Sussman, A. B., & Lukas, M. F. (2022). Understanding and neutralizing the expense prediction bias: The role of accessibility, typicality, and skewness. *Journal of Marketing Research*, 59(2), 435–452.

that's on human nature. We're imperfect. And companies have no choice but to sell to imperfect humans because there are no other kinds of buyers.

But where marketers can exploit and exacerbate these biases and judgment flaws are in promotions that help us underestimate the burden of debt we're considering. The tactic that most specifically exploits these biases are debt offers which delay payments for a period of time. This is something you see from automakers, furniture stores, and other sellers of more expensive goods. "No payments for six months!"

It's a compelling incentive that stimulates demand – get stuff now, figure it out later. But in the process of "figuring it out," the prospective borrower is likely to make gross miscalculations about the affordability of payments. He/she is likely to imagine making or having more money when the payments would start and have a significant underestimation of what other expenses will also need to be paid.

WHAT YOU CAN DO

You will see a discussion of a variety of biases in this book. Most biases are unconscious. And these biases affect our judgment specifically because we don't know we have them. As a result, the people who have the strongest biases are those that think they have no bias at all. This is because they're not monitoring for the bias and correcting themselves when they detect it. So, just understanding that you have this bias is an important first step.

Another effective way to combat a bias is to seek examples that counter what you're thinking.[9] This tactic is used in racial debiasing programs to combat stereotypes. A stereotype is thinking that is incomplete and/or...well...lazy. People relying on stereotypes have either not had the opportunity to learn, or taken the time to consider, the complexities of a topic, a challenge, or a group. The

---

[9]Gocłowska, M. A., Crisp, R. J., & Labuschagne, K. (2013). Can counter-stereotypes boost flexible thinking? *Group Processes & Intergroup Relations, 16*(2), 217–231.

trick is convincing people to do the difficult work of challenging their own assumptions.

If someone believes a stereotype about a group of people, thinking of members of that group who don't fit that stereotype helps open that person's mind. For example, if someone thinks all Californians are hippies living in communes, they should think of all the hard core capitalists and captains of industry from that state. Such an exercise helps a person to gain a more complete (and complex) picture of things.

The biases we're discussing in this book are related to your ability to afford a loan. Specifically, many of us are biased toward thinking we're going to have more money and fewer expenses in the future. To avoid falling into such a trap, try to think of times in your life when you had sufficient – or any – discretionary income to deal with new expenses. If you can't think of many – or any – then it should help you understand what your future is likely to hold.

In this process, you may find yourself thinking, "Well, I've never had money left over at the end of the month, but I'm sure it will different in the future." If you're thinking that, chances are things won't be different and that loan may not be affordable.

But, if you:

- Are in a place where you are able to put some money away every month.

- Are using a loan to verifiably reduce your expenses (like taking out a new mortgage that replaces a more expensive mortgage or rent).

Then there's a good chance that the debt makes sense! Again, the goal of this book is not to keep you from ever taking out a loan. Debt and credit are necessary staples of modern life. The goal of this book is to help you avoid taking on too much debt or loans that are either beyond your budget or unnecessarily expensive. Thinking of counter examples is an effective means of doing that.

4

SELF-CONTROL FAILURES

The stereotype of someone struggling with debt is of a person who lacks self-control. He or she wanted things beyond their budget, so they buried themselves in debt to rock a nicer wardrobe, car, or house than they could otherwise afford. While the overall picture of debt is more complex than that, we're all probably guilty of engaging in retail therapy when we shouldn't have. Our self-control breaks down. We give in to impulse.

When are we most likely to suffer self-control breakdowns? When we're tired, confused, or otherwise feeling spent. Often, if we think back to uncharacteristic purchases made or words said to others, we remember feeling exhausted at the time.

Decisions related to debt are complex and exhausting. Whether it's deciding to take out a new loan, or buying something on credit now that you would not be able to otherwise afford, chances are that type of decision drains not only your physical resources, but mental as well.

For example, let's consider the decision to take out a credit card. Credit cards – like other forms of debt – have lots of moving parts – prices/interest rates, payment due dates, incentives like "travel miles," escalation clauses, penalties, and more. Odds are that no two credit card offers are going to match each other attribute-for-attribute.

Offer 1 will be better in some ways, while Offer 2 will be better in others. And, if you take the time to examine the two offers top-to-bottom (which you *absolutely* should), you're likely to end up tired and confused – with scrambled eggs in the part of your head where your brain used to be. It's a recipe for making bad decisions. Plus, it makes us more likely to give into impulses. Here's why that is and how marketers take advantage.

TRADEOFFS

What makes debt-related decisions so difficult and potentially treacherous is that they involve tradeoffs. You give up on one goal (at least temporarily) in order to achieve another.

For instance, if you have a goal of home ownership, you *could* methodically save your money for 15–30 years and pay cash for the house in order to meet your other goal of living debt-free. But 15–30 years is a long, long time. You want to own a home now. Plus, you have to live *somewhere* during those 15–30 years and that somewhere is going to charge you rent – which will likely cost more than a mortgage.

But, on the other hand, owning a home also means owning its problems. And, as any homeowner will tell you, there are *always* problems. Basements flood. Roofs leak. And, in the instance my house, half the honey bees in town could decide to build a network of hives throughout your ceiling. (Expensive to fix, but we did get a free jar of honey from the bee keeper.) Just being able to call your cranky landlord to take care of any repairs has a certain appeal to it.

And then there's the decision between different types of mortgage loans. As mentioned, no two loan offers are going to be exactly alike. So, then you have to weigh the tradeoffs between the various attributes of the loans you're considering.

The goal of home ownership is nearly universal and a key component of the venerable American Dream. As you can see, it comes with a host of complications and conflicting goals. After carefully calculating the above-mentioned tradeoffs (and many others), you decide to abandon your goal of living debt-free to meet your goal of home ownership. You now have a mortgage. Congratulations! Enjoy the yard work.

Shopping for and purchasing a home comes not only at a financial cost but a cognitive one as well. Research shows that calculating tradeoffs like these are among the most difficult decisions we can make. And if calculating these tradeoffs doesn't make your life difficult enough, it can also wreck your self-control which, in turn, might lead to a cascade of poor decisions both related to the house purchase and beyond.

AN OUNCE OF MENTAL RESOURCES FOR EVERY POUND OF GOALS

The limitations humans face are not just the previously mentioned limits on our mental capacity for judgment and decision-making. We have constraints – often tight ones – on all our resources. But these constraints are tightest on the resources of time, money, and energy.

Further complicating matters, we have a seemingly unlimited supply of needs and desires. And these needs and desires extend far beyond just material possessions. We want to love and be loved, to be a good person, to be knowledgeable, skilled, kind, generous, respected, successful, and more. And meeting *all* these goals with such tight constraints... it's just not possible.

As we have so many goals competing for so few resources, we are forced to make tradeoffs.[1,2] The t-word is quite possibly the ugliest word in the English language... at least when it comes to our mental state. We, as a species, HATE tradeoffs.

While we have a general feeling for what a tradeoff is, let's define it explicitly. Tradeoffs mean having to choose from an array of desirable options but which are desirable for different reasons. There is no obviously superior option. If there were, it would be easy.

WHEN OUR BRAINS RUN OUT OF GAS

Choosing among roughly equivalent options is inherently difficult. And, when you are weighing tradeoffs in hopes of making a

---

[1]Miller, G. A. Galanter, E., & Pribram, K. H. (1960). The integration of plans. In G. A. Miller, E. Galanter, & K. H. Pribram (Eds.), *Plans and the structure of behavior* (pp. 95–102). Henry Holt and Co.
[2]Kruglanski, A. W., Shah, J. Y., Fishbach, A., Friedman, R., Chun, W. Y., & Sleeth-Keppler, D. (2002). A theory of goal systems. *Advances in Experimental Social Psychology, 34*(2), 331–378.

choice, this means meeting some goals while abandoning others. That hurts us.

Or, more specifically, it depletes us.[3] "Deplete" is the word researchers use to describe a draining of mental resources. It's as if our brain's battery is running on low. And we need our mental resources for just about everything – analyzing information, making decisions, or even just functioning in a socially acceptable way.

While supermodels and rock stars may be able to act as unrestrained divas, the rest of us have to make some effort to get along with others. Axl Rose can show up 4 hours late for a concert or bite someone he doesn't like without consequence.[4] But you and me? Not so much. We need to remain vigilant about saying "please," "thank you," and – most especially – not biting people whenever possible. It helps us make our way in the world.

Making our way in the world helps us achieve *goals*. We have a lot of those. Achieving any of those goals will require the help and/ or approval of others. And behaving like a barbarian makes that less likely. Even Justin Bieber has had to apologize for things for fear of having his goals undermined by public disapproval.[5]

So, before you give in to road rage because someone cut you off in traffic, remember that giving in to such an impulse comes at the cost of longer-term goals (like avoiding jail, not getting sued, and maintaining a driver's license among others).

THE COST OF SELF-CONTROL

We "exercise" or "exert" self-control so that others will want to help us, or at least engage with us, in the future. It's called exercise or exertion because it requires a significant amount of effort. It's

---

[3]Wang, J., Novemsky, N., Dhar, R., & Baumeister, R. F. (2010). Trade-offs and depletion in choice. *Journal of Marketing Research*, 47(5), 910–919.
[4]Kaufman, G. (2006, June 27). Axl Rose release from jail after bar brawl, leg-biting incident. *MTV*. https://www.mtv.com/news/2dq65i/axl-rose-released-from-jail-after-bar-brawl-leg-biting-incident. Accessed on March 20, 2023.
[5]Spanos, B. (2015, November 10). All apologies: 22 times Justin Bieber said 'Sorry'. *Rolling Stone*. https://www.rollingstone.com/music/music-news/all-apologies-22-times-justin-bieber-said-sorry-41634/. Accessed on March 20, 2023.

draining. And when we get drained/depleted, it reduces our self-control and changes our judgments and decision-making for the worse.

And the self-control you exert on one thing can impact your trying to exercise self-control on something entirely different. For example, let's say your refrigerator is making an annoying buzzing sound and the repair person can't get there until tomorrow. That buzz is annoying enough that you feel an irrational but understandable urge to scream at your refrigerator.

Not wanting to appear obviously insane in front of your family as they eat their breakfast, you suppress the urge to curse at the demonic appliance pushing you to the brink. You exercise self-control and get on with your day as best you can. Good for you!

But will the amount of energy you expend not screaming at your refrigerator in the morning affect a decision you might be making later that afternoon? Probably. Suppressing a strong urge is going to heavily tax your mental reserves to the point where they won't be as readily available to you later that day. In all likelihood, you are going to find it harder to conjure the thought and self-control needed for certain decisions following your bout with the refrigerator buzz.

A number of studies have shown that the mental resources required to overcome one urge makes a person less likely to resist the next. For example, participants in one experiment who were asked to suppress a thought ("Don't think about white elephants.") drank more alcohol later that day.[6] Another experiment showed that people tempted with – but forced to resist – fresh-baked cookies were then less likely to complete cognitive tasks moments later.[7] Still another experiment showed having a contentious interaction with someone (where people had to suppress the urge to scream at each other) led to greater emotional outbursts later on.[8]

---

[6]Muraven, M., & Shmueli, D. (2006). The self-control costs of fighting the temptation to drink. *Psychology of Addictive Behaviors*, 20(2), 154.
[7]Baumeister, R. F., Bratslavsky, E., Muraven, M., & Tice, D. M. (2018). Ego depletion: Is the active self a limited resource? In *Self-regulation and self-control* (pp. 16–44). Routledge.
[8]Vohs, K. D., Baumeister, R. F., & Ciarocco, N. J. (2005). Self-regulation and self-presentation: regulatory resource depletion impairs impression management and effortful self-presentation depletes regulatory resources. *Journal of Personality and Social Psychology*, 88(4), 632.

Getting depleted not only affects our decision-making ability but other things related to our cognitive function. It makes us more tired, cranky, indecisive, impulsive, and depressed.[9]

DEPLETION AND HOME BUYING

Because there are no clearly "right" choices, tradeoffs are the hardest type of decision we can make. Ever shopped for a house or apartment? Grueling. And depleting. There's going to be multiple houses that aren't clearly superior or inferior to one another. And you have to make what will likely be the most important purchase decision of your life from an array of roughly equivalent options.

Never bought a home? Even if you've just watched one of those home buying shows, you get a sense of what we're talking about. These "reality" (read: fake) shows feature couples with behavioral tics, unrealistic budgets, and nothing in common – especially when it comes to priorities in selecting a house. Person A wants to live close to work at a greater expense, while Person B wants to live further out from the city so they can afford more space. Person A wants a modern style of architecture while person B wants a classic style.

Even contemplating these choices make your head spin as you try to weigh these varying attributes. Each option meets some goals while abandoning others. Yet, we watch these shows because there is no right answer. You can endlessly debate which option the couple should choose.

If you've ever shopped for a house, it's a similar exercise except instead of three options, there are 300. And instead of four or five silly attributes, it's dozens of important ones that can significantly affect your quality-of-life. These include affordability, structural integrity, crime rates, quality of school systems, proximity to work, and so on. Calculating these tradeoffs takes *everything* out of you.

It's not because we're indecisive – though some people do have an easier time of making decisions than others. It's because buying a home is an important and difficult choice. The home-buying

[9]Baumeister, R. F., Faber, J. E., & Wallace, H. M. (1999). Coping and ego depletion. In C. R. Snyder (Ed.), *Coping: The psychology of what works* (pp. 50–69). Oxford University Press.

decision involves a seemingly infinite number of tradeoffs to be calculated. And the depletion resulting from calculating these tradeoffs may well degrade the subsequent decisions about purchasing and financing it.

HOW MARKETERS OF DEBT DEPLETE YOU...

Many of the factors we discuss that lead to depletion are inevitable facts of life. Dealing with difficult people. Resisting the urge to eat an entire sleeve of Oreos. These are common and ever-present.

But, as consumers, we do find ourselves in scenarios where we're either being intentionally depleted or presented with a decision when our mental reserves are likely to be at their lowest.

If you've ever gambled at a casino, you've likely experienced free alcohol showing up at your table when you're playing. While a free martini may feel celebratory in the midst of a hot streak, the casino's intent is transparent: to degrade your decision-making and encourage you to take bigger risks than normal.[10] Many of us could probably derive the casino's intent there. But here's the catch: Even just the act of offering the gambler a drink, and the mental resources it may take that person to resist it, will deplete the gambler and degrade their decision-making.[11]

Marketers of debt have similar tactics – to introduce add-on expenses once the buyer is depleted from the process of buying or financing something. And one of the most unnecessarily tiresome or depleting purchases you can make is a car.

Case Study: Buying a Car

The process of buying a car usually *starts off* fun. Test-driving. Considering colors and interiors. Daydreaming about trips you

[10]Lane, S. D., Cherek, D. R., Pietras, C. J., & Tcheremissine, O. V. (2004). Alcohol effects on human risk taking. *Psychopharmacology*, *172*, 68–77.
[11]Muraven, M., & Shmueli, D. (2006). The self-control costs of fighting the temptation to drink. *Psychology of Addictive Behaviors*, *20*(2), 154.

could take or all the attention your new ride will attract. Then the work starts.

After calculating the tradeoffs and deciding on a make and model, then negotiating a price with the dealer, you're already depleted. And, turns out, your work has just begun.

As about 84% of new cars are financed, chances are you must now begin the arduous task of negotiating terms of the auto loan – 4, 5, or 6 years with each carrying a different interest rate and monthly payment.[12] Then there's the presentation of all the taxes, title issues, and things you thought that were included but aren't, like floor mats. A couple of hours in, it's virtually guaranteed that your head is spinning and your judgment is slipping.

It is at this point that the add-ons start being pitched to you. After first having gone on at great length about the reliability of the car to get you to agree to the purchase, the sales person starts discussing all of the potential and crushingly expensive repairs you could encounter with this new car. Failed electrical systems. Cracked axles. Engine replacement. If any of these [highly improbable] things happen to your new car, you could be on the hook for thousands of dollars.

The salesperson then attempts to sell you extended warranties, service plans, and road side assistance services as an antidote to these long-shot, nightmare scenarios. Many of these items cost hundreds – if not thousands – of dollars. As mentioned, you are already depleted, so your judgment is not optimal and your resources for resistance are strained.

Further complicating matters, refusing these expensive supplementary items would be easier if you had to write a check for their entire cost upfront. But you don't. When rolled into your loan, such offerings may cost $50–$100 per month.

Even if you find the resources to refuse, the salesperson will ask you multiple times to reconsider. Each refusal depletes you further, making it harder to refuse the next item.

---

[12]https://www.statista.com/statistics/453000/share-of-new-vehicles-with-financing-usa/

This scenario is not unique to cars. Many products have add-ons (typically in the form of some kind of extended warranty) that we have to decide on at the point of purchase – after we have expended the mental resources on choosing what to buy.

What can we do to resist getting sold something we don't really want or need when we're depleted?

- *Defer the decision:* If you feel pressured to make a decision but you're not sure what to decide, don't decide. Tell the salesperson "no" for now but ask if you can come back if you change your mind. You often (actually, almost always) can. And the ability to reconsider under better circumstances – with more internal resources and less external pressure – will almost always lead to better decision-making.

  It's worth noting that deferring a decision is not always the wisest course of action – something we will touch upon in the next chapter. But the difference in this instance is *external pressure*. When we are faced with making a difficult decision, we avoid doing so, if given the opportunity.

  But when under time pressure to decide – such as when that car salesperson is trying to get you to buy an extended warranty – that dynamic reverses.[13] We become more likely to make a decision, often to our own detriment. And many deadlines being pushed by a sales person are artificial. They're typically marketing/sales tactics designed to force a decision on the spot.

- *Take a break:* If you're struggling to process a decision because you lack energy or understanding, take a break. Come back at it when you're feeling better. Get something to eat or drink. Take a nap. Go for a walk. Meditate. Pray. Clear your mind. Do the things that boost your energy and/or spirits.

---

[13]Dhar, R., & Nowlis, S. M. (1999). The effect of time pressure on consumer choice deferral. *Journal of Consumer Research*, 25(4), 369–384.

- *Give yourself a pep talk:* Research has shown that how depleted you believe yourself to be affects your ability to exercise self-control.[14] In other words, if you're wallowing in how exhausted you feel, your self-control and decision-making are going to reflect that. Similarly, if you tell yourself that you feel pretty good and can handle the decisions, it should help you.

---

[14]Clarkson, J. J., Hirt, E. R., Jia, L., & Alexander, M. B. (2010). When perception is more than reality: The effects of perceived versus actual resource depletion on self-regulatory behavior. *Journal of Personality and Social Psychology*, 98(1), 29.

5

WHEN WE ABANDON OUR GOALS

I'm sick of following my dreams. I'm just going to ask them where they're going and hook up with them later.
– Comedian Mitch Hedburg[1]

As mentioned in the last chapter, tradeoffs require us to abandon one goal in order to meet another. That hurts. Given that any rational adult knows at some level that we can't get everything we want, it probably *shouldn't* hurt. But it does. Now, the way a fully rational being would deal with trading off one goal for another would look something like this:

- *Step 1: Prioritize wants and needs.*

- *Step 2: Allocate time, money, and energy appropriately to the highest priority goals.*

- *Step 3: As resources are used up, gracefully concede that some of your lesser goals will not be met in order to accomplish something more important.*

- *Step 4: Pat yourself on the back for a job well done.*

---

[1]Mitch Hedberg Quotes. (n.d.). *BrainyQuote.com*. https://www.brainyquote.com/quotes/mitch_hedberg_297471. Accessed on November 4, 2024.

Such a process requires the intellect, maturity, and realism to understand that we cannot have it all and that sacrifices have to be made. In other words, this is not something we tend to do.

It's not just navigating tradeoffs that we find difficult. In the weighing of current and future goals – instant gratification versus long-term fulfillment – we sometimes make choices that seem ridiculous upon later reflection. We eat the donut instead of having a smoothie. We binge watch 20 years of Simpsons™ episodes instead of studying for the exam. Or, in the context of this book, we run up debt in the short-term rather than adhere to our long-term financial goals.

Now a motivational speaker or Peloton instructor might tell you to "dig deep" and "crush all the barriers" to achieving your goals – that you can have everything you want if you work hard enough. Yes, we do succeed in making certain sacrifices and trade-offs. But, not all of them. Not even close.

Every CEO, world-beating entrepreneur, or other person who achieved some tremendous goal still struggles with – or more likely, avoids – dealing with tradeoffs in their daily lives. Even though these people are outliers of professional achievement, they are still human.

Many of the CEOs and entrepreneurs with whom I've talked are grateful for their hard-earned professional success. But at the same time, they recognize it was at the expense of more time with friends, family, or non-business pursuits. It's not that they didn't value loved ones or cherished past times. It's that their days are 24 hours just like anyone else's and at some point, something has to give.

How do humans deal with the pain of recognizing that we cannot meet some of our goals? By convincing ourselves that we are not abandoning a goal, but just delaying it. After all, it's not abandoning a goal if you tell yourself you're just going to meet that goal at some other (later and indefinite) time. And research has shown that the more important the goal or decision, the more we delay dealing with it.[2] And we do this regardless of whether that delay is obviously detrimental to our situation.

---

[2]Krijnen, J. M., Zeelenberg, M., & Breugelmans, S. M. (2015). Decision importance as a cue for deferral. *Judgment and Decision Making*, 10(5), 407–415.

Psychologists refer to this as *choice deferral*. The more difficult a decision is, the more likely we are to avoid making it.[3] Which decisions are the most difficult? Choosing among options which are both attractive – such as choosing between two goals.

Intuitively, we might think avoiding difficult decisions or choices would be stressful or frustrating as unresolved issues mount. But the truth is choice deferral often makes us feel better and more hopeful about the choice with which we're grappling.[4] Remember how optimistic we tend to be about the future? Well, it seems that when we push difficult choices off to that optimistic realm known as the future, we somehow think we'll have better luck figuring things out at a later date. (We won't!)

In other words, we pretend the conflict doesn't exist in hopes that things will get better as time passes. We rationalize. This should feel familiar to just about all of us – rationalizing. And there is probably nothing we rationalize about more than why we can't meet (or start to try to meet) our long-term goals today.

- I'd quit smoking, but it's a stressful time (as if there are any periods of time that are stress-free).

- I'd lose weight but the holidays are coming up (as if in January we will no longer be either tempted by ice cream or repulsed by the idea of doing sit-ups).

When we make these rationalizations, we are being fully sincere. At least in the moment. We insist that we're not abandoning our goals, just delaying them. Many of us will tell ourselves that the choice of a new hot tub for the house does not run in conflict with our goal of financial independence. Instead, we'll take the hot tub now, assuring ourselves that long-term goals will be dealt with later.

---

[3]Tversky, A., & Shafir, E. (1992). Choice under conflict: The dynamics of deferred decision. *Psychological Science, 3*(6), 358–361.
[4]Wei, H. L., Hai, C. Y., Zhu, S. Y., & Lyu, B. (2021). The impact of consumers' choice deferral behavior on their intertemporal choice preference. *Frontiers in Psychology, 12*, 555150.

LOSS AVERSION

The phenomenon described above relates to a psychological principle called "loss aversion," also known as Prospect Theory.[5] Loss aversion at its most simple says that when somebody has a chance to realize a small but certain gain today, they are likely to do so, even at the expense of forgoing a larger gain in the future.

Conversely, when someone is faced with a loss today, they avoid it, even at the likelihood of having to face a bigger loss in the future. We tend to defer difficult things in hopes that they become easier or less expensive in the future – even though they often become more difficult or costly as time passes (looking at you personal finance, weight loss, and climate change).

In other words, we hate losing much more than we love winning. And like a classic Greek tragedy, our disdain for losses often causes us to lose bigger and win smaller. We sell winning stocks too early and losing stocks too late. And we keep gym memberships despite having not worked out in 18 months.

The *smart* thing to do is to recognize the loss early and move on from it. The *likely* thing to do is grit our teeth and – against all available information – insist that things are going to turn around.

In terms of money decisions, it means we have the tendency to be penny-wise and pound-foolish. Here are some common behaviors that result from loss aversion:

- A tendency to purchase products that have a lower initial price but a higher cost of ownership. We buy a house because it has a lower price even though it has no insolation, functional kitchen, or HVAC system. The house's purchase price is $50,000 less than others you considered, but it's going to require $150,000 to make it livable.

- Executives placing an over-emphasis on cutting expenses (vs. increasing income or revenue), slashing marketing budgets in times of difficulty, worsening the effects of a difficult market.

---

[5]Kahneman, D., & Tversky, A. (1979). Prospect theory: An analysis of decision under risk. *Econometrica*, 47(2), 263–291.

- Giving up on long-term gains to avoid short-term losses like a tech company slashing its research and development budget to make this quarter's profit targets.

- Prioritizing immediate gains (travel miles/cash back, etc.) of a transaction over long-term costs (monthly payments or ultimate debt levels).

- Buying those terrible, expensive, and often useless extended warranty programs for products because we feel it protects us from loss.

While loss aversion is common, its influence on our choices and behavior vary according to personality and context. The loss aversion bias is strongest in those with the least experience and understanding of a particular type of decision. This jives with Robert Cialdini's excellent – and very enjoyable – book on persuasion.[6] Cialdini's book talks about "persuasion triggers" – seemingly small rationales, rules, or stereotypes we often rely upon to form opinions or make decisions.

And when can a trigger have the greatest effect? When the person being persuaded has little-to-no base of knowledge about a topic. It makes sense once you hear it. Getting an expert to change his/her mind about that topic is difficult. But someone who is a blank slate? Not difficult at all.

If someone wanted to influence me about either organic chemistry or cross-stitching, they're going to be able to do so easily. I don't have the first idea about either. So, if I was in a store shopping for a cross-stitching set, that sales person is going to have an above-average chance at overselling me. If I had a working base of knowledge, I'd be able to refute the salesperson telling me I needed $500 worth of materials (instead of $10–20) to get stitching. Instead, the likelihood is that I'm getting soaked for platinum-plated stitching needles.

When we encounter something but don't understand it, we look for something – anything – to help make sense of it. And, often

---

[6]Cialdini, R. B. (2006). *Influence: The psychology of persuasion* (Revised ed.). William Morrow. Seriously, great book and an easy read.

times, we are left relying on emotional reactions or pre-conceived notions or biases. Rules-of-thumb. Stereotypes. "Gut" feelings.

As a consumer, it could be as simple as looking at two similar items and assuming the more expensive one is of higher quality. As a human being, it could be seeing people or cultures unfamiliar to us and becoming agitated or uncomfortable. In either case, it is an instance of choosing to be uninformed or misinformed rather than doing the difficult and draining work of learning about a complex topic.

Personal finance ranks with nuclear physics in terms of things that people generally don't understand and would like to avoid learning about if they can help it. And, while 99.9% of people can have a blissful life being oblivious to nuclear physics, the same can't be said about personal finance. No matter how hard you try, personal finance is going to enter your life and force you to make decisions about it.

Since most of us have little understanding of personal finance, we can be left grasping for something to tell us what to do. In the case of personal finance, the "something" we find is often loss aversion – the feeling that, no matter what, we don't want to lose money or spend more than necessary. The feeling is so strong, we interpret this emotion as information or insight. But, it's not. It's a form of anxiety that results in a bias. And like any bias or thing that makes us afraid, it blinds us to the wider world without our realizing it. It prevents us from being either thoughtful or informed about a topic before acting. This results in poor behavior and decision-making.

Given that humans have a common and powerful bias – loss aversion. How do marketers of debt take advantage? A lot of it takes the form up upselling borrowers forms of insurance related to either the debt itself, or the thing being bought with the money being borrowed (like a house), including:

- Life, disability, mortgage insurances to protect payment of a mortgage.

- Home warranties (which are just another form of insurance).

- Fees to secure lower interest rates.

- Promotion of fixed rate refinance options when interest rates are headed lower.

- Mortgage refinance packages that gouge consumers with fees and lost equity in favor of a slightly lower mortgage rate.

What can you do to overcome loss aversion? Here are four easy steps:

1. Take a deep breath.

2. Learn more about the debt you're considering.

3. Seek advice from a trustworthy person who knows more about finance than you.

4. To borrow from Darth Vader, search your feelings. If you're still feeling stressed or conflicted about a particular debt decision, you probably don't know enough about it yet.

Since loss aversion is a bias or fear based out of a lack of understanding, your challenge is to gain understanding. As discussed, most of us avoid learning about finance when given the chance. But learning about finance does not mean getting a master's degree or doing calculus. It could mean reading some articles online or asking a friend who has a stronger background in the area than you.

Another great way to inform yourself is getting competitive offers. It may not give you a complete understanding of a particular loan, but it will help you understand if the first offer you got has fair prices and terms. The Internet makes this incredibly easy.

Seriously, if you want to see a look of pure ecstasy, tell a mortgage broker that you haven't looked at other sources of financing for the house you've decided to buy. That broker is about to get a nice bonus from signing you up for an overpriced loan.

There are more resources at your disposal – and you will have an easier time becoming informed – than you realize. If you can take a little extra time to understand the booby traps of certain debt, it will serve you immensely well. As a borrower, you have two abilities that shift power from the lender to you:

1. Being informed.

2. Being willing to walk away when you know or even suspect that a deal might not be right for you.

As a consumer, these are your super powers. Even just giving a slight flex of either power will force your lender to be fair with you. Using either of them will save you money, decrease your anxiety, and help you make better decisions.

6

OUR INCONSISTENT MINDS

Consistency is contrary to nature, contrary to life. The only completely consistent people are the dead. – Aldous Huxley[1]

If there were any logic to the English language, "consistency" would be a four-letter word. Consistency is the art of applying a set of rules or principles the same way across a variety of contexts. This, in turn, should yield behavior that is reflective of those principles every single time. It's exhausting just typing that. Every... single... time. Whew! I may need to lay down for a bit.

If you are looking for a reason why computers continue to replace more and more of our daily tasks and responsibilities, it's consistency. Hardware and software can accept and execute a set of instructions – without deviation or exception – every single time (Unless there's been a recent Windows™ update.[2]).

Human beings, on the other hand, not so much. Consistency is hard! As humans, we get tired, moody, anxious, and bored. And all of these things affect our judgment and decision-making, which makes

---

[1]Huxley, A. (1929). *Do what you will: Essays.* Chatto & Windus.
[2]Rim shot.

43

consistency a herculean challenge. To be consistent, you have to take into account:

- what your values are;
- what decisions you've made in the past;
- what you would need to do in the present circumstance to remain in keeping with your past actions and stated values.

If it sounds like a lot of work, that's because it is. This is particularly the case when you multiply this process by the massive number of money-related decisions we have to make every day. It's more than most (any?) of us can do. Even just the number of debt-specific decisions we make on a daily basis are seemingly limitless:

- When I spend money, should that purchase go on credit?
- When I receive money, should I pay down a credit line?
- Should I open, transfer, or close a credit line?

The chance that we can be consistent in all of these decisions is virtually nil. And that lack of consistency gave birth to an important area of study known as mental accounting.

MENTAL ACCOUNTING – YOUR INTERNAL BOOKKEEPER APPEARS TO BE HEAVILY CONCUSSED

Mental accounting is the study of our furiously inconsistent interactions with money developed by Nobel prize–winning economist Richard Thaler.[3]

As we discussed, loss aversion looks at the big picture of how we treat gains differently than losses. Mental accounting takes the next step. It details how we internally categorize and process various losses (spending money) and gains (receiving money) in our heads. Each loss or gain we experience is unique in its own way – timing, context,

---

[3]Thaler, R. (1985). Mental accounting and consumer choice. *Marketing Science*, 4(3), 199–214.

amount, etc. And because they feel differently or exist in different contexts, we react differently – often hilariously so – to them. If I had to put money on which theory explains the most of our goofy/strange/ disastrous financial decisions, I'm placing my bet on mental accounting.

EVERYBODY HURTS (WHEN PARTING WITH CASH)

A good example of our inconsistent nature – and one that deals directly with debt – is the difference between paying cash for purchases versus using a credit card. For most people, spending $500 cash in a single day would hurt. And by "hurt," I mean that nagging tug at the part of your conscience attempting to be fiscally responsible. That tug is stronger when spending cash than swiping a credit card. Even though the loss is the same regardless of our method of payment, the loss feels much different depending on your method of payment.

Pulling a bunch of cash out and handing it over to the cashier hurts. It makes us acutely aware of the depletion of our financial reserves and any long-term goals we may be abandoning or delaying as a result of this transaction. Not only does it make the transaction unpleasant but it also diminishes our enjoyment of whatever it is we're buying.[4]

If an expenditure is a loss, with a cash transaction you experience that loss more acutely, for a longer period of time, and more often thanks to the number of actions involved in the transaction. These actions include handing the cash over, making/receiving change, taking inventory of the cash remaining (which gives you a sense of ALL of your expenditures for the day), and possibly returning to the ATM to get more cash. This makes a significant impact on you psychologically. Those cash losses loom larger than if you used a credit card. You end up feeling poorer and less responsible with cash. The pain and sacrifice associated with a purchase are even

---

[4]Prelec, D., & Loewenstein, G. (1998). The red and the black: Mental accounting of savings and debt. *Marketing Science*, 17(1), 4–28.

more memorable than with credit.[5] As a result, subsequent cash purchases become more difficult.

Credit cards feel better and are less "painful" than spending cash. You swipe that card and trust the credit gods are taking care of things. There is less friction, and the loss is less tangible. It can feel a bit like an all-you-can-eat buffet, except you're not going to feel grotesque at the end of it – at least not until you get your credit card statement. To compound things, paying with credit cards also makes you less price sensitive, with some people being willing to pay twice as much for something as when they pay with cash.[6]

And a "No payments for 6 months!" financing plan... well that feels positively divine. With no immediate or near-term sacrifice related to the acquisition of a good, that item feels like a gift or a prize. You can enjoy the good with fewer strings attached or tugs at your conscience.

Making matters even more scary, if you are one of the 43% of US Adults that have their credit card loaded on their phone, studies have shown that you can forget about a consumer feeling any pain or discomfort when making purchases.[7] Users actually experience a feeling of pleasure.[8] And that feeling of pleasure equates to a higher frequency of purchases.

It's counter-intuitive. Spending cash *should* feel better than swiping a credit card. With cash, you are not taking on any long-term obligations or incurring the extra expense of interest being charged. You're spending what you have, not what you don't. In most contexts, it's the more responsible choice. Less guilt. Fewer future ramifications. And yet... ouch.

---

[5]Soman, D. (2001). Effects of payment mechanism on spending behavior: The role of rehearsal and immediacy of payments. *Journal of Consumer Research, 27*(4), 460–474.

[6]Prelec, D., & Simester, D. (2001). Always leave home without it: A further investigation of the credit-card effect on willingness to pay. *Marketing Letters, 12*, 5–12.

[7]Statista. (2024). Share of smartphone users who use proximity mobile payments in 23 different countries worldwide in 2019 and 2021. https://www.statista.com/statistics/244501/share-of-mobile-phone-users-accessing-proximity-mobile-payments-country/. Accessed on July 24, 2024.

[8]Wang, M., Ling, A., He, Y., Tan, Y., Zhang, L., Chang, Z., & Ma, Q. (2022). Pleasure of paying when using mobile payment: Evidence from EEG studies. *Frontiers in Psychology, 13*, 1004068.

With credit card purchases? You are a well-oiled spending machine without the slightest hint of friction to rouse the fiscally responsible part of your conscience. That lack of friction also carries over to the choices you make, where people paying on credit have a tendency to buy more impulsive or unhealthy items.[9]

WHEN SPENDING CASH FEELS GOOD

But does that mean the act of spending cash is *always* painful? No. It depends on how we came upon that cash and how we categorize it. As we take in money, we associate different labels and purposes for that money. As Thaler explains, we form different accounts or categories in our heads for different pools of money.[10] This, despite the fact that your bank account is just a single [smaller than you would like] pot of money for the purpose of meeting a wide variety of financial commitments.

For example, sometimes we run into "found money." Remember when we talked about "irregular expenses?" Found money is irregular income. This is money that was not part of our regular working income and that we tend to treat differently than other money we receive. Often, we treat found money as "fun money" – something we should spend immediately on something we enjoy.

Let's say your Nana or Grammy sends you $100 for your birthday. You are more likely to treat it as fun money for a couple of reasons. First, because you think "that's what Grammy would want." And you're right. She *would* want you to have fun with it. Good ole Grammy.

But second (and more importantly), this is no ordinary money Grammy has sent you. Not at all. This is birthday money. In your mind, it cannot and should not be used to pay bills. Sure, you may be close to having your power turned off. And, your car makes a

---

[9]Thomas, M., Desai, K. K., & Seenivasan, S. (2011). How credit card payments increase unhealthy food purchases: Visceral regulation of vices. *Journal of Consumer Research*, 38(1), 126–139.
[10]Thaler, R. H. (1999). Mental accounting matters. *Journal of Behavioral Decision Making*, 12(3), 183–206.

really strange sound – and gives off an even stranger odor – whenever you hit the accelerator.

Too bad. The time for practicality was before that sweet, sweet birthday money arrived nestled inside of a birthday card featuring a basset hound with a noise maker hanging out of its mouth (so cute!). Now, you have a mandate for fun. You can figure out how to power your appliances or repair your car issue some other time. And, if Grammy sent you the $100 in cash or a gift card, there is no friction or pain associated with spending *this* cash on ice cream and video games.[11] In fact, you may very well spend it faster than if she had sent you a check. This cash, unlike the cash we described a few paragraphs earlier, is burning a hole in your pocket due to the "type" or category of money it is (birthday money) and the format in which it was received (cash or gift card).

The example of birthday money is admittedly silly. But only a little. Birthdays, after all, are supposed to be fun. And, too often, we categorize money as "found money" or "fun money" when it really isn't. Yes, ice cream and video games are fun. But you know what else is also fun? Having electricity and a working car! I'm pretty sure Grammy would agree. Yet, we are more inclined to indulge when getting money in such a context.

A more common example would be getting a refund for a good or service that was not ultimately provided. A lot of times we will treat it as a windfall even though that's an absurd notion.

Tax refunds are a great example. You get an unexpected check from overpaying your taxes (because who really understands their taxes?). Suddenly, you look around and notice all the sales on flat screen TVs that are happening in late April and realize that your 60-inch TV is really too small and that your favorite show is really only enjoyable on screens 80 inches or larger.

All last year, chances are you looked at the money being held from your paycheck for taxes and thought bitterly, "But I've got bills to pay!!" Now, that same money has returned home to you. And rather than welcoming it home to the safe sanctuary of your

---

[11]Helion, C., & Gilovich, T. (2014). Gift cards and mental accounting: Green-lighting hedonic spending. *Journal of Behavioral Decision Making*, 27(4), 386–393.

savings account or paying those bills, you are hot with a spending fever that will only subside until you have procured the largest TV on the market. Same money, two very different feelings. What was once "hard-earned" money "needed to pay bills" on the front end has become fun money on the back end.

Seemingly inconsequential factors in our dealing with money can have significant effects on how we spend or save. And our responses to different contexts related to losses and gains are not just psychological. We have physiological responses to them as well. Research has shown people's hormonal levels change in response to losses, gains, and perceived changes in financial status like how wealthy or poor we feel in a given moment.[12] And those physical responses further influence behavior going forward. In fact, even just the denominations (large bills vs. small) of money being handled can determine the strength of these physiological responses.[13]

HOW MARKETERS EXPLOIT OUR INCONSISTENCIES WITH MONEY

If there is an easy target for debt marketers, it's consumers' inconsistent interactions with money. Our collective lust for "found money" makes rewards, cash back, and other forms of rebates very compelling purchase incentives. As we will get into greater detail later in the book, these "rewards" are so miniscule and compel us to actually pay so much more in interest, they make no financial sense. But, they *are* fun. Much in the way you convince yourself that a Mega Millions™ ticket is a sound investment when the jackpot gets north of $500 Million, you imagine all the ways you're going to spend money from these rewards. And, visions for using credit card rewards have about as much of a chance as working out as your visions for winning the lottery.

---

[12]Dinsmore, J. B., Stenstrom, E., & Nepomuceno, M. V. (2022). Testosterone and financial risk-taking. In *Handbook of experimental finance*. Edward Elgar Publishing.
[13]Stenstrom, E., Dinsmore, J. B., Kunstman, J., & Vohs, K. D. (2018). The effects of money exposure on testosterone and risk-taking, and the moderating role of narcissism. *Personality and Individual Differences*, *123*, 110–114.

Here are some of the most common ways marketers exploit our deficiencies in mental accounting:

- "Cash Back" *Credit Cards & Travel Miles:* I tell you what... Why don't you make $1,300 in purchases which you'll be paying high interest on for years and, in exchange, I'll give you between $13 and 26? What's that you say? Sound like a terrible deal? It is!

- *Refunds/Rebates on Purchases:* You see this for cars very often. Purchase a $40,000 car which will be financed through the manufacturer for five years and get $500 in cash back. You could just apply the $500 to the balance, but in all likelihood you'll spend it on Yosemite Sam™ mud flaps and floor mats for the vehicle. By the way, in all likelihood, you're going to be paying $6,000 or more in interest on that vehicle.

Both of these examples play with our inconsistent mental accounting as well as how we treat money in the present differently than money in the future.

HOW YOU CAN BE MORE CONSISTENT WITH YOUR MONEY

Is there a way to become a Certified Mental Accountant (CMA)? Sadly, no such certification currently exists. But it should. Being able to master the art of mental accounting would not only save us from excessive debt, but enable us to enjoy our lives (and our purchases) more fully. If we were certified mental accountants, we would make wiser spending decisions and feel better about the times where we do treat ourselves. But until the American Accounting Association joins forces with the American Psychological Association to offer a CMA certificate, this chapter will have to suffice.

Here are some simple habits to help break ourselves of some of our more absurd financial inconsistencies and be liberated from the long-term chaos of overconsumption.

Pre-Payment: You know what feels better than buying with credit? Getting something *after* you have paid for it. While it may frustrate your itch to acquire something immediately, it will help you enjoy the product more over the long-term. Researchers from MIT (Drazen Prelec) and Carnegie Mellon (George Loewenstein) extended the mental accounting framework to look at various levels of pain experienced in different payment scenarios. And, what they found is that paying in advance for something makes that item more satisfying and enjoyable. At the point where you get your hands on the item, there is no sacrifice to be made and no contemplation of future obligations. That item is yours. *Really* yours.

If you have ever gone to an all-inclusive resort, you know the feeling. You can eat, drink, water ski or do whatever else without the constant ticking of a meter in your head tabulating the cost of the vacation. It is a way to know (and cap) your expenditures for a vacation. And it is also a good way to have a carefree and painless week of rest and relaxation.

No doubt, it is impossible to pre-pay for *everything*. And a primary reason that credit exists is that we can't afford to pay for certain things needed in the moment. If you can pay in advance for some things, you will find it not only improves your credit but also your enjoyment what is being bought.

Do Not Consider the Source of Income When Deciding What to Do With It: A recurring theme in mental accounting research is how we tend to allow prior events and judgments to dictate current decision-making criteria. We become either snake-bitten or emboldened by past occurrences that should have no basis on our current situation. The earlier example of tax refunds is a prime example. A tax refund should not be treated any differently than any other source of income. Yet, come March and April, retailers report a lift in consumer spending when people start to get their refunds.[14]

Autodebit For Savings: There are a number of things we all know we need to save for: retirement, college for kids, rainy day fund, holiday gifts, etc. And, in general, we feel guilty about not doing a better job of saving. With all of the things in life that constantly

---

[14]Rosenbaum, E. (2023, April 12). Tax refunds are getting smaller, and fit into the picture of a slowing economy. *CNBC*. https://www.cnbc.com/2023/04/12/how-tax-refunds-that-are-getting-smaller-fit-into-a-slowing-economy.html. Accessed on May 8, 2024.

need to be paid for, setting aside money for the future is very difficult. The difficulty of doing this is magnified by the accounting gremlins in our heads.

Having a certain amount of money automatically diverted from our paychecks to these savings accounts is a great way of avoiding having to go through the pain of parting with money every month. If the money never hits your checking account, then you don't feel the pain. Social Security, IRAs, 401k's, and pensions are effective for this reason. Money for retirement is not put in possession of the individual, so they don't have to muster the will power to part with it. Because of this, people stay in these programs and save more as a result.[15]

---

[15]Benartzi, S., & Thaler, R. H. (2013). Behavioral economics and the retirement savings crisis. *Science*, *339*(6124), 1152–1153.

SUMMARY ONE

We've covered some ground here, so let's recap:

- **Despite being stretched for resources (time, money, and energy) in the present – and at almost any time we can remember in the past – we [erroneously] think we will have more resources in the future than is likely.** This biases us toward gratification in the present at the expense of our future well-being. When marketers use tactics such as delaying payments on items, it further exploits that bias by putting us in a future mindset that makes us believe things are more affordable than they are (Intertemporal Discounting and Slack).

- **We have way more goals than resources to achieve them. Meeting one goal often comes as a tradeoff in not meeting another. Calculating these tradeoffs depletes our intellectual resources and self-control in the moment.** The very nature of many financial decisions – in particular, getting something today at the expense of paying it off it the future – involves many large and complex tradeoffs. Navigating such a complex series of tradeoffs can make us disposed toward impulsive or ill-considered decisions. When marketers of expensive goods like cars put customers through long, complicated purchase processes and then try to sell add-on goods and services, it exploits this dynamic (Goal Abandonment, Tradeoffs, and Depletion).

- **Humans hate losing more than they love winning. This is especially true when contemplating gains and losses of money. Because we feel stronger about losses than gains, it often leads us to make suboptimal financial decisions.** We go too far in avoiding losses – often causing us to lose bigger down the road (in the case of investments) or in paying for unnecessary "loss prevention" services (like warranties, guarantees, and insurance) (Loss Aversion).

- **And, just to make things positively chaotic, we categorize income and expenses differently in our minds that causes us respond to those inflows and outflows in varying (and often irrational) ways.** Spending feels different in different contexts which, in turn, affects our subsequent judgments and decision-making. Because buying on credit feels better – is less "painful" – than using cash, we are predisposed to taking on debt (Mental Accounting).

7

LIFE IS HARD, BUT MATH IS HARDER: UNDERSTANDING THE PRICE OF THINGS

When talking about financial products, just about the only criteria for purchase is price. Bank A's money spends just as well for you as Bank B's. And since pretty much all banks have online payment portals and comparable customer service, there's not much else that sets them apart. So, your choice of lenders likely comes down to who can give you the best price/interest rate.

Sound simple? It's not. Because:

- Interest rates change every day.

- Compounding interest is difficult to understand.

- Though we think most debt comes with a single price (interest rate), they actually come with multiple prices.

- Those various prices will come in different forms and be called things other than "price," such as late fees, processing charges, loads, points, and more.

- Many of those prices will change over the life of the loan or be introduced *after* you have agreed to the terms of the loan.

- Lenders will scatter their multiple prices across their marketing materials making it more difficult to get a sense of the loan's true cost.

Each of these factors exploits a common cognitive weakness or blind spot for consumers. This spells trouble for consumers trying to make optimal financial decisions or even understand what a loan is truly costing. In other words, if you find figuring out the cost of a loan difficult, that's because it is. In the next few chapters, I'll show you why that can seem intentional on the part of lenders and how it confuses us.

AN INTRODUCTION TO PRICES

As we delve into all the ways that the pricing of debt confuses and misleads us, it's first important to get a sense of what prices do and how people interact with them. The key to not getting taken in by deceptive or misleading pricing practices is confidence, patience, attention to detail and... boy, we are in soooooo much trouble. Kidding! The truth is that there are elements of pricing that fool all of us at one time or another. And for a variety of reasons.

A big part of my "day job" as a marketing professor is researching how different levels, forms, and presentations of prices affect consumer judgment. It may sound sad and depressing, and... maybe it is. But not to me! When you realize how slight changes in an aspect of a price can change people's perceptions and resulting choices, it makes things a lot more interesting.

Prices exert enormous influence on the decisions and behaviors of people, businesses, and governments everywhere you look. It's not just something that affects a balance sheet. Many – perhaps most – riots and wars have been started as a reaction to, or in anticipation of, prices of necessities like food, water, and energy. So, before you dismiss the topic of pricing as mundane, let's consider the impact of prices and price presentation on your life.

WHAT A PRICE DOES

Most commonly, when we think of the word price, we think of it as a standard of exchange. Put more simply, it's how much a seller requires in order to give the buyer something. You want a mocha-lattè-chino-poopoo from Starbucks™. Starbucks says you can't have it until you meet their standard of exchange. You dutifully give them the $43 and pint of blood they require, and an exchange is made. BOOM!

We encounter a seemingly endless number and array of prices every day. Yet, we hardly ever contemplate all the things that prices do, reflect, and communicate. Let's say you went through the trouble of setting up a lemonade stand. That involves a number of things such as acquiring ingredients, making the lemonade, schlepping the lemonade and components of the stand (table, chairs, signage, pitcher, cups) out to the street corner of your choosing. Finally, and perhaps most importantly, you need to set a price for the lemonade.

You set the price at two dollars per glass. It may seem a routine decision, but it's something that sets a number of things in motion. In setting this price, it reflects your belief that you understand your costs and how many glasses you'll likely sell. You believe $2 per glass will not only cover costs but generate enough revenue to be worth the time, money, and energy you dedicated to this venture. And, if people driving by your stand are hesitant to stop and buy your lemonade, you may reduce your price to $1.50. When you do, you are likely to see cars that would have previously driven right past you suddenly stop and order.

Perhaps two dollars per glass *will* be enough to get people to stop and buy. Then, ideally, you'll profit handsomely. Or, maybe you've underpriced. And, if that's the case, you might end up losing money because you didn't realize your actual costs are $2.50 per glass (this is some gourmet refreshment you're selling!). Or perhaps you don't become the tycoon you could have because you didn't realize the world would have paid five (FIVE!!!!) dollars a glass for your extraordinary lemonade.

Whatever the case, just setting the standard for this exchange (two dollars per lemonade) has an enormous impact on the ultimate success of your venture. It's a complex and powerful thing, this pricing. Price your product one way and people buy. Set a different price and people drive right past your stand.

Setting a price for something is a seemingly basic and necessary decision in any business venture. As the business owner, the price reflects your understanding of the business and your beliefs about the market. That's on the seller's side. What about the buyer's side?

HOW CONSUMERS INTERACT WITH PRICES

For consumers, a seemingly endless number of factors affect not only how fair or unfair you perceive the price to be but what that price is telling you about the product. Seeing the price of a product causes us to make a lot of assumptions about it. The price also sets our expectations about what the product should be and how much we think we'll enjoy it. If the price is high, we assume it is of optimal quality, limited supply, and should be compared with high-end competitors.

Or, perhaps we view the price as being *unfairly* high. Typically, an unfair price feels like an act of aggression by the seller. It can enrage us. Perhaps we come across a lemonade stand where a kid wants TEN DOLLARS(!!!!) for his lemonade. We see the cheap paper cup containing the lemonade. Then, we notice the very faint coloring of the beverage inferring little actual lemon juice is in it. From this we may assume the purveyor of the lemonade is taking advantage of extremely warm weather to push some low-quality sugar water at an unreasonably high price. Who needs that nine-year-old and his overpriced lemonade?

On the other hand, if the price is low, we assume the lemonade is "good enough" and in ample supply. And paying such a low price may make it easier to enjoy the lemonade. Even if it tastes like rusty tap water, we may tell ourselves, "What else were we expecting at that price?" and think we got a good (or at least, reasonable) deal.

This is known as the price = quality heuristic (aka "You get what you pay for."). We use such a heuristic or rule-of-thumb because knowing enough about all the things we have to pay for is hard. Actually, it's impossible.

Because it's impossible, we look for something – anything – to tell us what we should do. And when we don't know what to think about a product, price often becomes our first, and sometimes only, point of focus. In the absence of significant product knowledge, we take price as a signal of information about the product – well beyond how much money you have to give up to get it.

Because we have so much experience with prices, our minds are databases of previously seen or experienced prices called *reference prices*. These reference prices give us a standard by which to judge newly encountered prices. And even if we struggle to remember our kids' names from time-to-time, our mental pricing database is both strong and dynamic. Because of this, we rarely (if ever) fail to have a judgment, feeling, or inference about the price of an everyday item.

For example, we understand that a bottle of water typically costs $1.50–$2.00 from a vending machine but significantly more at a concert or sporting event. This helps us not physically threaten the nice lady at the concert concession stand when she tells us the bottle of water is going to cost $8. Our database of reference prices tells us that's the going rate at events like these. And, though the price is exorbitant, our database advises us to avoid causing a scene with the nice lady who's just doing her job. So, we just pay the $8 like every other poor shnook at the show.

Even if we don't know what a given thing should cost, we find some point of comparison from which we can attempt to judge value. If you've never gotten lemonade from a lemonade stand before, you won't be able to draw on a reference price specific to that context. Instead, you will likely compare the $2 price to lemonade at a restaurant or convenience store. Or, if you've never bought lemonade anywhere before (weird, but we all have our quirks), you may compare the $2 price to the soda or other beverage that you commonly purchase. From those comparisons, we come up with a judgment of value – is this thing worth what I'd have to give up in order to get it?

Similarly, if your wealthy aunt told you she was buying you a $200,000 car, you would immediately make certain assumptions about the [AWESOME] style and quality of the car. If she told you she was buying you a $3,000 car, you would make a separate set of [modest] assumptions.

These assumptions aren't always correct. But, in most of our experiences as consumers, we have found that more expensive things are often nicer and vice-versa. As a result, we feel safe in making these assumptions. And, typically, things more or less work out, even if not to the last penny.

The prior examples of pricing for cars and lemonade are as simple as it gets. There is one price for one product. While there are many features and options for a car, the core offering – a machine that will take you places – is known. Plus, you can easily get a sense of relative value by searching prices for that vehicle at competing dealers.

And, though you can always negotiate on car prices, the bottom line list price of the car provides a frame of reference for similar products at that cost.[1],[2] Weighing or prioritizing which brands, models, or features you prefer may prove challenging. But comparing the cost of the vehicles will be easy.

THE COMPLEX NATURE OF DEBT PRICING

But, dear reader, we are here to talk about debt, not cars or lemonade. The examples of cars and lemonade – even with all the factors affecting our perceptions of their prices – are relatively simple. There's one clear price for that product. You pay the price and the transaction is complete.

But the price of debt is *not* simple. At all. And where we often get into trouble as consumers is that debt pricing has all the features of the best movie villains in that it's:

- Complex and mysterious.

- Multi-dimensional/has multiple components.

- Reveals significant new risks/dangers/abilities over time.

---

[1]Don't get me started on "no haggle" car dealerships. They really should be called "no discounts for people afraid to negotiate" dealerships.
[2]I suppose you could negotiate with the nine-year-old on lemonade, but just give him the $2 for God's sake. It's cute.

In other words, RUN FOR YOUR LIVES! Marvel's next villain to take on the Avengers™ should be called the Debtonator™ who convinces Earth's mightiest heroes to take out credit cards and mortgages.[3] Then, the Debtonator springs lots of hidden fees and escalating interest rates on them. Man, that Hulk™ is toast. I can hear him now: "Hulk would smash but Hulk need to go drive Uber™ to make minimum monthly payment on credit card." Poor Hulk.

The common fallbacks we use to assess the value of something – like reference prices and price transparency – don't apply to loans. Interest rates change *every* day. Lenders are constantly coming up with new ways to present their pricing – despite regulations designed to specifically prevent this.

The next few chapters will go into detail about aspects of debt pricing that boggle our minds. Sometimes, like trying to understand compounding interest rates, our minds are boggled because the price is not intuitive. Other times, our minds are boggled because the lender does things to make the true cost of a loan harder to understand. In either case, just familiarizing yourself with these common borrower mistakes and biases should empower you to get a better deal on your loans.

We'll break down components of debt pricing and show how our intuitions and biases hurt our understanding of these prices. Then, we'll look at how marketers of debt exploit these cognitive shortcomings.

---

[3]Trademark 2022, Me. Pay me, Kevin Feige.

8

MISUNDERSTANDING INTEREST RATES

Most immediately, when thinking about the price of debt we think of interest rates. While the concept of an interest rate is familiar, it is a price that is in a different form than any other price we encounter.

Every other price we see is a fixed amount of currency, like $2 for a lemonade. But pretty much any interest rate we encounter is a percentage of the amount borrowed that is charged – and *compounded* – over time. These are difficult things to wrap your brain around when you're talking about a 30-year mortgage or a credit card that has an *infinite* timeline.

Plus, in the instance of all credit cards and some mortgages, that interest rate also frequently changes. Therefore, knowing how much you're going to pay on a loan could be literally impossible to calculate.

As we've discussed, well-reasoned decisions about anything in the future are challenging. But now you have to take into account this alien form of pricing? It's not surprising that nearly half of borrowers admit to not understanding interest rates.[1] And many of those that think they *do* understand them are actually mistaken.[2]

---

[1]Lee, J., & Hogarth, J. M. (1999). The price of money: Consumers' understanding of APRs and contract interest rates. *Journal of Public Policy & Marketing, 18*(1), 66–76.
[2]Raynard, R., & Craig, G. (1993). Estimating the duration of a flexible loan: The effect of supplemental information. *Journal of Economic Psychology, 14*, 317–335.

The whole comparison process we went through with cars and lemonade earlier isn't really available to us on debt products. Prices on consumer staples like lemonade are relatively stable. When those prices rise, they typically go up very gradually over a long period of time. When I was kid, a drink from a vending machine cost 50 cents. Now, it's $1.50. Not too bad when you consider we're talking about 30 or 40 years difference between the two prices.

But interest rates are not stable. They change *every day*. And when you're talking about an interest rate that is compounded (more on that in a minute) over a long period of time, little changes have a big effect on how much you're paying. When you add to this that finance companies often obscure the true interest rate being charged (see "Price Transparency" chapter), the borrower is at a real disadvantage. So how can we judge pricing on a loan?

TRYING TO MAKE SENSE OF INTEREST RATES

Given our lack of understanding of interest rates, the fact that they are in constant flux, and a considered effort by some lenders to make rates harder to understand, what do we do to get a sense of the cost of our loans?

First, most consumers focus on the monthly payment of the loan to gauge affordability.[3] On the one hand, framing the cost of a loan in terms of your monthly budget makes a lot of sense. You definitely want to still be able to afford the rent on your apartment after taking out a loan. On the other hand, when consumers look at a monthly payment they *drastically* underestimate the amount of that payment that is interest.

Second, borrowers are left to evaluate interest rates relative to similar loans available at that time. We look for a reference price. For example, let's say we go to a loan brokerage website like LendingTree™ and are shown multiple offers for a mortgage. If the site offers us a choice between a 30-year mortgage at 6% versus one

---

[3]Renuart, E., & Thompson, D. E. (2008). The truth, the whole truth, and nothing but the truth: Fulfilling the promise of truth in lending. *Yale Journal on Regulation*, *25*, 181.

at 7%, it's an easy choice. The lower price (6%) is better, so we choose it.

Congratulations! We're not totally crazy or stupid. (What a relief!) But, in all likelihood, we're still not really sure what it means, other than we got a competitive rate – at least relative to that one other loan. We still don't really know what we're paying.

If you take out a mortgage of $200,000 at 6% interest, what does that mean? Intuitively, we might assume that 6% of each payment would be comprised of interest. We'd then calculate in our heads that, over 30 years (360 monthly payments), we would pay $12,000 in interest on top of $200,000 we borrowed. This would result in a monthly payment – before taxes, insurance, utilities, Home Owners Association (HOA), or other fees – of $589, with $33.33 going toward interest and the rest paying down the balance of the loan.

If we assumed this, we would be embarrassingly wrong. Our intuition had us calculate a *flat* interest rate, not a *compound* interest rate. Flat interest rates are intuitive while compound rates are not. Also, flat interest rates appear to only exist as a concept in textbooks, not in the market place. Compounding interest is what is charged on any commonly used loan.

A flat interest rate is applied *once* on a loan. Compounding interest is *continuously re-applied* throughout the life of the loan. As interest is charged on your loan and added to the balance, the interest rate is then applied again to that new balance. And again. And again. And again.

In searching for our $200,000 mortgage, we go to a bank website that will break down the loan for us. Once the bank website tells us we will be paying about $1,200 per month, not $589, we begin to understand that interest may not work the way our intuition was suggesting. Additionally, what the website won't tell you explicitly is that you'll be paying about $432,000 total for your $200,000 house. It also doesn't mention that the designation of which dollars count toward interest and which count as principal will change over time. What the...?

Even once you vaguely come to terms with the notion of compounding interest, it still defies intuition. For example, you are likely to assume that every monthly payment consists of the same amount of principal and interest. And if you make that assumption, you will be seriously (and expensively) wrong.

If interest and principal *were* constant throughout the loan, for every $1,200 payment you made, about $555 would count toward the principal of the loan and $645 would go toward interest. That's still a shocking amount of interest, especially when you started with an assumption of a flat interest rate. Now, the loan probably doesn't seem like such a great deal. Six percent sounds like such a small number. If you're paying 6% on a loan, why is 54% of every payment going toward interest?

And, the truth is, the deal is actually much worse than that. Because the bank decided that 54% was clearly not enough (wait... what?!?!), it weights the loan with more interest up front. As you'll see below, the initial payments for that mortgage will actually be about 83% interest.[4]

Typically, your payments for the first 20 years of a mortgage are mostly interest while payments in years 20–30 are heavily principal. And, given that the average homeowner stays in a house about 18 years, guess what that means?[5]

- People are going to be paying off their mortgage at a much slower rate than they probably realize.

- The bank makes extra money while you pay the loan, because it's mostly interest.

- The prior point enables the bank to make more money when you *sell* the house, because there will be a higher balance on the mortgage that has to paid off at settlement.

OK mortgage companies, we're starting to get the idea. This is kind of a one-way relationship.

---

[4]The mortgage industry will, no doubt, say, "But the good news is that interest is tax deductible!" That's like someone breaking your leg and then saying, "You lucky duck! You're about to get a tour of your local hospital!"
[5]ipropertymanagement. (2021, November 12). Average length of homeownership. *Property Management*. https://ipropertymanagement.com/research/average-length-of-homeownership. Accessed on September 20, 2022.

For example, here is a year-by-year breakdown of interest versus principal payments for that $200,000 30-year mortgage at 6% interest. Known as an *amortization table* – this exhibit shows the timing of loan payments and how much of each payment goes toward interest and principal.[6] Notice that it's not until year 19 of the mortgage where your mortgage payments are allocated more toward principal than interest (Table 2).

Table 2. Interest Versus Principal Payments Over the Life of a Home Loan.

Year	Interest Paid	Principal Paid	Remaining Balance
1	$11,933.19	$2,456.02	$197,543.98
2	$11,781.71	$2,607.51	$194,936.47
3	$11,620.88	$2,768.33	$192,168.14
4	$11,450.14	$2,939.08	$189,229.06
5	$11,268.86	$3,120.35	$186,108.71
6	$11,076.41	$3,312.81	$182,795.91
7	$10,872.08	$3,517.13	$179,278.77
8	$10,655.15	$3,734.06	$175,544.71
9	$10,424.84	$3,964.37	$171,580.34
10	$10,180.33	$4,208.89	$167,371.45
11	$9,920.73	$4,468.48	$162,902.97
12	$9,645.13	$4,744.09	$158,158.88
13	$9,352.52	$5,036.69	$153,122.19
14	$9,041.87	$5,347.34	$147,774.85
15	$8,712.06	$5,677.16	$142,097.69
16	$8,361.90	$6,027.31	$136,070.38
17	$7,990.15	$6,399.06	$129,671.31
18	**$7,595.47**	**$6,793.74**	$122,877.57
19	**$7,176.45**	**$7,212.77**	$115,664.81

---

[6]https://www.amortizationtable.org/

Table 2. *(Continued)*

Year	Interest Paid	Principal Paid	Remaining Balance
20	$6,731.58	$7,657.63	$108,007.17
21	$6,259.27	$8,129.94	$99,877.23
22	$5,757.84	$8,631.38	$91,245.86
23	$5,225.47	$9,163.74	$82,082.12
24	$4,660.27	$9,728.94	$72,353.17
25	$4,060.21	$10,329.00	$62,024.17
26	$3,423.14	$10,966.07	$51,058.10
27	$2,746.78	$11,642.43	$39,415.67
28	$2,028.70	$12,360.51	$27,055.16
29	$1,266.33	$13,122.88	$13,932.27
30	$456.94	$13,932.27	$0.00

Lenders understandably avoid flaunting the amount of interest you'll be paying. After all, it would be bad business to hear your loan officer say, "Once you sign off on this baby, I'm gonna get that boat I've always wanted." Even so, this information *is* easy to find – if you know where to look. But we typically don't look. It's unpleasant to consider. We are left to our intuition, which as we've just discussed, is NOT up to the task.

But it's not just that interest rates are counterintuitive. There are other reasons we are terrible at understanding rates.

EXPONENTIAL GROWTH BIAS

Consumers regularly demonstrate a lack of understanding of compounding interest rates, something referred to by researchers as "exponential growth bias."[7] Exponential growth is a term we feel we understand. But let's get into its precise meaning. Think of

[7]Stango, V., & Zinman, J. (2009). Exponential growth bias and household finance. *The Journal of Finance*, 64(6), 2807–2849.

"exponential" as the opposite of gradual. For example, when companies grow, they often grow gradually, perhaps at a rate of 5 or 10%. But sometimes, particularly with early-stage tech companies, a company will experience exponential growth when their product goes viral. They might grow 50, 100, or 200% in a year.

Consider the below chart of Amazon's stock price from years 2000–2022 (Fig. 2). If you think of a stock price as a reflection of people's belief about a company's future earnings, you can see something happen around the year 2015. Investors belief in Amazon's future earnings began to grow exponentially. The rise in price went from a straight line at a gradual incline to a steep curve. That curve marked the beginning of exponential growth.

Similarly, when you chart compounding interest, it also exists on a curve. Our intuitions conceive of it as being a flat line (Fig. 3). Look at the amount of interest paid from the amortization table provided earlier in this chapter.

The curve of the line shows the amount of interest paid behaving exponentially. The loan is heavily loaded with interest up front. Our intuition would have predicted the amount of interest being paid as being flat or constant. Instead, it's twisting and turning.

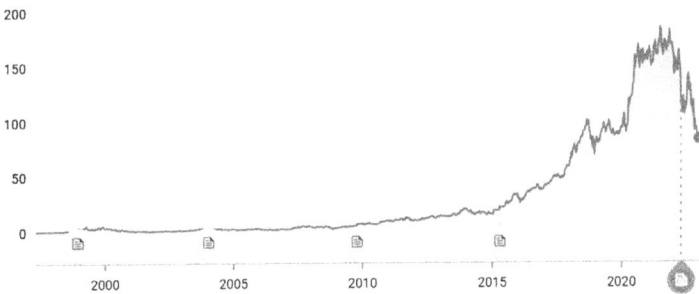

Fig. 2. Example of Exponential Growth.[8]

Exponential growth bias reflects a lack of understanding of the nature of compounding interest. On the debt side, this means borrowers don't understand how much interest they're paying over

[8]Finance.google.com, Amazon stock price search conducted January 6, 2023.

$15,000.00

$10,000.00

$5,000.00

$0.00

Fig. 3. Interest Paid Annually Over 30 Year Mortgage.

the life of the loan – or even in an individual payment. They think the debt is cheaper than it actually is. On the investment side, it means a household is unlikely to understand the benefits of saving early and often to earn long-term, compounded interest. This bias costs households dearly on both sides.

As is the case with so many biases, people are unaware and resistant to the notion they might have skewed judgment. Not only that, but they're deluded and overconfident about being knowledgeable and objective. Because of this, those that need the most help or education on the topic are the least likely to seek it.[9] Instead, they stumble along needlessly costing themselves money.

NUMBERS MAKE US ANXIOUS

Fear is the mind-killer.[10]

– *Frank Herbert*

Part of the reason is that compounding interest is math-related. "Math anxiety" is a real and widespread phenomenon.[11] We know

[9]Levy, M. R., & Tasoff, J. (2017). Exponential-growth bias and overconfidence. *Journal of Economic Psychology, 58,* 1–14.
[10]Herbert, F. (1965). *Dune.* Ace Books. (Original work published 1965)
[11]Foley, A. E., Herts, J. B., Borgonovi, F., Guerriero, S., Levine, S. C., & Beilock, S. L. (2017). The math anxiety-performance link: A global phenomenon. *Current Directions in Psychological Science,* 26(1), 52–58.

from experience that stress makes it harder to analyze and remember things. Many of us have pulled an "all-nighter" to study for an exam only to freeze-up when taking the test. Things that we've known forever become hard to remember in the moment. Momentary stress blocks our access to knowledge or cognitive capabilities we normally could take for granted. Problems we're normally comfortable solving become more difficult.

Anxiety tends to make us less thoughtful or thorough. It makes it harder to learn new things or remember the things we've already learned.[12] As a result, we often jump to ill-considered conclusions when stressed.

It's not surprising, then, that anxiety about math encourages us to avoid numbers. But it goes beyond task avoidance. Brain scans (fMRIs) of people with high levels of math anxiety have shown that math-related tasks activate "threat detection" centers of the brain. It was as if those subjects were being chased by a tiger.[13] Those with high levels of math anxiety may even feel physical pain when confronted with a math-related task – as if being bitten by that [imaginary] tiger.[14]

What does this mean for understanding the cost of debt? Nothing good. As mentioned, most people don't understand how interest rates work. They're also likely to avoid seeking an understanding due to their discomfort with the complex topic. In fact, research has shown that the better a person understands how interest works, the less likely that person is to buy something on credit.[15] Or, put differently, borrowers have less of an understanding of how loans work than non-borrowers. Yikes.

Instead, these lesser informed borrowers will likely tell themselves that they *do* understand something they clearly don't, stumbling recklessly into a long-term financial commitment. This greatly increases probability of:

---

[12]Robinson, O. J., Vytal, K., Cornwell, B. R., & Grillon, C. (2013). The impact of anxiety upon cognition: Perspectives from human threat of shock studies. *Frontiers in Human Neuroscience*, 7, 203.

[13]Researchers did not mention anything about a tiger. That's just my illustration/metaphor.

[14]Lyons, I. M., & Beilock, S. L. (2012). When math hurts: math anxiety predicts pain network activation in anticipation of doing math. *PloS One*, 7(10), e48076.

[15]Disney, R., & Gathergood, J. (2013). Financial literacy and consumer credit portfolios. *Journal of Banking & Finance*, 37(7), 2246–2254.

- Not understanding what they're actually paying.

- Paying more than they should.

COGNITIVE LOAD

Another reason is that, when buying a house, there are so many things to get done and think about, concepts like loan amortization never occur to us. And the more things weighing on our minds, the less able we are to perform analysis or solve problems. Researchers refer to this as "cognitive load."

Our brains can only process so much, so the more we ask of it, the more likely the quality of our judgment and decision-making is to suffer. Much of our discussion in this chapter has centered specifically on the quantitative element – interest rates. And analyzing an unfamiliar and uncomfortable topic like compounding interest represents a high cognitive load to the prospective borrower.[16]

But the debt decision involves a lot more than math. We have to consider goals, tradeoffs, predict our future circumstance, and more. The complexity, unfamiliarity, and emotionality elements all increase cognitive load in their own way, challenging a person's ability to make the best decision for themselves.[17]

And when overwhelmed with a myriad of considerations, we pick one or two things upon which to focus.[18] We *have* to simplify. Not because we don't want the ability to consider everything and make all of our own choices. We absolutely do want these things. But, we have limits in our ability to process all of these criteria. Freedom of choice can be invigorating. It can also

---

[16]Sweller, J. (1988). Cognitive load during problem solving: Effects on learning. *Cognitive Science*, 12(2), 257–285.
[17]Trémolière, B., Gagnon, M. E., & Blanchette, I. (2016). Cognitive load mediates the effect of emotion on analytical thinking. *Experimental Psychology*, 63(6), 343.
[18]Malone, T., & Lusk, J. L. (2017). The excessive choice effect meets the market: A field experiment on craft beer choice. *Journal of Behavioral and Experimental Economics*, 67, 8–13.

make us miserable.[19] And, when the number of options and considerations exceed our ability process them, the likely outcomes are:

- Becoming paralyzed by the situation and do nothing.

- Delaying decision-making.

- Simplifying our decision-making. Essentially, we perform a cognitive coin flip where complexity is eliminated for the sake of remaining within the bounds of our abilities and well-being.[20] As with other instances where we've flipped a coin to decide a scenario, this reduces a complex situation to single – and potentially arbitrary – factor.

In this case, the point of focus is likely the size of the monthly payment, not what is actually being covered in that payment. And there are a million rationalizations you can invoke – everybody else is doing it, that's just how mortgages or car loans work, etc. Plus, you get a house or a car out of the deal, so it's not like it's *all* bad.

The point of this is not to make you depressed or angry. (Though it may.) It's not even to say that mortgages are scalding cauldrons of hidden fees and confusing pricing. (Though they are.) The point is that it's all very confusing and counter-intuitive and we don't really know what we're getting other than a house and a monthly payment. Compounding interest and loan amortization – two complex concepts that occur over a long period of time – go far beyond our intuition and understanding. Because of this, human beings are not well-equipped to fully grasp their consequences.

THE PRESENTATION OF INTEREST RATES

As we will get into in greater detail in the "Partitioned Prices" chapter, a lender has a lot of options in presenting an interest rate.

---

[19]Schwartz, B. (2015). The paradox of choice. In S. Joseph (Ed.), *Positive psychology in practice: Promoting human flourishing in work, health, education, and everyday life* (pp. 121–138). Wiley.
[20]Or "rock-paper-scissors" if you prefer.

Since the choice of loans is primarily a decision based on price, how a price is presented has enormous influence over whether or not a consumer decides to make a purchase.

For instance, if you are shopping for a new credit card, the direct mail, SPAM, or TV advertisement may offer a specific rate. Or, you may even be told it has a "0% introductory rate." That's on the advertisement.

But, when you dig in to the fine print, you will not get a plain interest rate. You will instead get a range of potential rates. Your rate is not, say, 20%. It's actually "Prime plus...15%." (Prime is the interest rate the bank pays to get the money to then lend to you.) This is the bank's way of saying the rate will fluctuate based on how much it costs them to borrow the money to then lend to you.

Raising prices to reflect your higher costs is fair enough. In a free-market economy, we don't expect the bank to lose money on our behalf. Banks don't give you an upfront price, because they can't. Their costs in lending you that money will change over time and those costs must be passed on to the consumer. All of that is reasonable.

But it does pose an extraordinary challenge to consumers. Unlike almost every other product or service out there, you don't pay a single price for debt upfront. Instead, you pay that price every month for as long as you maintain a balance on that debt. And that price is likely to change over time. Figuring out the cost of your debt requires not only understanding the price today but anticipating rate changes in the future.

This challenge also extends to mortgages where consumers have the option of choosing between loans with a fixed or adjustable rate. The fixed rate mortgage maintains the same rate for the life of the loan – if it's 6% in year 1, it will be 6% in year 30. The adjustable rate mortgage (ARM) typically has some initial period of a fixed interest rate (usually 5 years), followed by a period where the interest rate on the loan can adjust every 6 months.

Despite the inherent risk of a loan that can explode in terms of monthly cost, consumers often choose it. Why? Because consumers are usually approved for larger loans with an ARM that has a lower introductory rate than a traditional mortgage. But, inherently, this means that people are taking out larger loans than they would otherwise be able to afford.

It would seem that these riskier loans would be preferred by people with little credit or bad credit. And market data backs this up – ARMs are primarily the domain of the inexperienced or uninformed.[21,22] People with a lesser understanding of interest rates have a greater likelihood of choosing riskier mortgages. And once an inexperienced consumer decides to go with an ARM? They typically have no understanding of the mechanisms within the loan that might escalate the cost. As a result, they choose more expensive loans.[23]

WHAT YOU CAN DO

In the next chapter, we'll talk about how lenders make the cost of a loan harder to compare with other loans. But when it comes to becoming more savvy about how interest rates work, here are some of the things you can do:

- *Take a deep breath and relax.* Don't let math anxiety paralyze you before you even get started. Millions of people take out loans every day. You can do this.

- *Be honest with yourself about if you understand how the loan works,* what you'll paying, and if there are any mechanisms in the loan that will escalate your cost. If you're not sure, ask. Ask the lender. Ask a friend. Ask one of the many consumer finance advocacy groups out there. If your lender gets irritated or impatient with your questions, you need to find a new lender. That person is not concerned about your well-being.

- *Fire up the Google machine.* There are a number of tools out there to help you get a better understanding of your loan payments. A simple Google query for "Loan payment calculator,"

---

[21]Bergstresser, D., & Beshears, J. (1989). *Who selected adjustable-rate mortgages? Evidence from the 1989-2007 Surveys of consumer finances.* Harvard Business School Finance Working Paper No. 10-083.
[22]There's that recurring theme. The less experienced or informed are the most likely to get jammed on the cost of a loan.
[23]Lino, M. (1992). Factors affecting borrower choice between fixed and adjustable rate mortgages. *Journal of Consumer Affairs, 26*(2), 262–273.

"Amortization Table Maker," or "Borrowers Rights" will yield great resources to help you understand what you're getting into.

To quote the great Charles Bukowski, "The problem with the world is that the intelligent people are full of doubts, while the stupid ones are full of confidence." Be the intelligent person. Seek the information and help you need to make the best decision you can.

9

THE ILLUSION OF PRICE TRANSPARENCY

Perhaps one of the earliest lessons we learn about buying things is to "shop around." Regardless of what you're buying, being able to see prices of that good from multiple sellers will increase the likelihood of paying a lower price. It gives you power to extract a lower price from a seller who would otherwise not offer any discounts. The ability to see multiple prices of a good is known as *price transparency*. When you can see other prices – and sellers know that you can – sellers are forced to price competitively.

Price transparency is why the smartphone heralded an extraordinarily difficult time for brick-and-mortar retailers. Instead of having to drive to multiple stores to get a sense of value for a good, customers could merely reach into their pockets for their phones. Those devices gave consumers instant and total price transparency.

A consumer would walk into a Best Buy™ to look at – and more importantly *try* – laptops. Once that person had tried the laptops, had his/her kid get jelly-stained finger prints on all the floor models, and had a store employee answer 40 minutes of questions, the consumer decided on which model to buy. Then, the consumer would inevitably reach for his/her smartphone and do a quick online search for that product. Immediately, 25 competitive prices for that product appear. If the better price was online (and it usually was), the consumer would head home to order the product online, leaving behind a broken-hearted BestBuy sales rep and 30 jelly-stained laptops.[1]

This phenomenon is known as "showrooming" – a consumer using a store's facilities and inventory to make a decision on a purchase, but buying from some other retailer. You feel bad for Best Buy in that scenario. Or, at least, I do. They paid for the store, the inventory, and the sales associate to help the consumer figure out which choice to make. And with one search query, all of Best Buy's effort and investment is for naught. The sale instead goes to Amazon or some other online retailer.

But, at the same time, consumers *should* comparison shop. Not doing so is to invite (guarantee, really) getting gouged.

Price transparency takes financial power away from the seller and gives it to the consumer. It gives the consumer options and squeezes the seller's profit margin. And, in almost all of the products and services we buy, price transparency is easily accessible. But in finance? Not so much. We *think* we have price transparency, but it's actually an illusion.

Sure, you can find prices for loans. But you usually can't find *all* of the prices for a given loan in the same place. Plus, depending on the terms of your loan, the prices you *do* find may change after you have committed to the loan. That prevents borrowers from getting accurate and complete pricing information. As a result, borrowers have a lesser chance of finding the best deal. Let's look at how price transparency – or the lack thereof – hurts borrowers.

MUDDYING THE WATERS

Since consumers choose debt products almost exclusively on the basis of price, this means price transparency poses a significant threat for banks, especially in the Internet age. The price of a loan – or at least the perception of that price – is going to be the dominant factor in the consumer's choice of loans.

---

[1] If it makes you feel better, Best Buy and other retailers wisely started offering price matching guarantees to combat this practice. These guarantees get customers better prices without bankrupting Best Buy or its sales associates.

The Internet appears to give immediate price transparency on loans. A query to Google or a website like LendingTree™ can render multiple interest rates on the same type of loan product. This *should* pressure lenders to give discounts they'd rather not give. But before you start singing "Power to the People," you should know that what you're seeing is a mirage. And just like a person stuck in the desert who thinks he's found water, this price transparency will disappear the closer you look.

So, how does the bank pull this off?

Banks can't block people's access to the Internet. Banks also can't withhold their pricing from the Internet – if they do, they'll be cut out of the market completely. This really leaves only one option: obscuring the actual price.

As has been documented, some financial institutions intentionally complicate their pricing to fight price transparency and boost their profit margin.[2] In a perfect world, consumers would understand a loan's true cost and then be able to choose the best available option. Even though consumers usually fail to grasp the full ramifications of interest rates, they would still gain a sense of relative value. Choosing between 6% and 7% is easy. The buyer is going to choose the 6% loan every time.

But, if the lender at 7% can make its price appear to be 6% or better – without actually discounting their price? That's a highly desirable outcome for that bank. Since Bank A appears to have the lowest price, it gets the business. Bank A appears the cheapest without actually being cheapest. That's a win-win for Bank A. And by "win-win," I mean it's two wins for the bank (and a big loss for you). How can you make a higher price seem like a lower price? You can:

1. Find ways to present a price that makes it harder to compare to other prices. For example:
   - If your competitor advertises an annual interest rate, then advertise a seemingly lower (but actually higher) monthly rate.

---

[2]Carlin, B. I. (2009). Strategic price complexity in retail financial markets. *Journal of Financial Economics*, 91(3), 278–287.

- If your annual interest rate is outrageously high, advertise the amount of interest to be paid as a "fee."

2. Disperse some of the price into other fees or penalties so the loan has a 6% rate, but all the other "gotcha" items earns the bank 7% or more.

3. Present interest rates, prices, and fees separately (more on that in the next chapter) making it harder to understand the total cost.

4. Increase the use of technical language to make various price components more difficult to understand.

In general, these less-friendly lenders hide pricing components where they can. Or, if they can't hide the pricing in fine print or some remote page on a website, they use language that makes it harder to identify pricing components.

EXAMPLES OF REDUCING PRICE TRANSPARENCY IN DEBT

A good way to get a sense of deceptive pricing practices in debt is to look at [mostly ineffective] legislative attempts to curb these practices. And perhaps the biggest (and still mostly ineffective) law passed about this was The Truth in Lending Act of 1969 (TLA).

TLA dealt specifically with how lenders communicated the terms of their loans. The key provision forced them to communicate interest on the same terms, annual percentage rate (APR). "But wait," you say, "How else would lenders communicate interest rates?" As you'll see, the answer was (and still is), "In as many ways as would make someone more likely to borrow from them."

As you saw in the earlier chapter, interest rates defy intuition. A seemingly small number like 6% can mean tens or hundreds of thousands of dollars in interest. Most consumers aren't aware of this. But for those who *are* aware, there is still a challenge when lenders make numbers more difficult to compare – either by:

- Going from an annual rate to a daily or monthly rate (resulting in a smaller percentage rate being presented to the consumer).

- Converting the annual rate into a one-time fee.

TLA was designed to reduce this by forcing lenders to all communicate interest in an APR format. Getting prices of loans communicated in the same terms comparing ("apples to apples") makes them more easily comparable. And when we can compare prices in the same terms, we can make better choices. That was the goal of the legislation, but it was not the result, because what TLA doesn't do is:

- Stipulate that interest can *only* be communicated as APR.

- That the APR must be the rate communicated most prominently.

This means that lenders can still bury the APR in its materials so it's hard to find and still lead with a deceptive presentation of interest. Even if you're appropriately skeptical as you read the lender's promotional materials, you are likely to be influenced by those skewed numbers displayed most prominently.

WHY WE TAKE THE FIRST INFORMATION THAT COMES ALONG

So, why are we influenced by the first information we encounter? To reduce uncertainty. Humans lead a highly complex and uncertain existence. And for many of us, the need to reduce uncertainty – to bring closure to issues burdening us – is profound.

Known as an "anchoring effect," people have a tendency to be more persuaded by the first information they encounter.[3] We are intuitively familiar with anchoring effects when it comes to our initial evaluations of people. Language, dress, or other social signals we deem either impressive or inappropriate prompt us to make snap judgments about the whole of a person, to form a "first impression." From a t-shirt with a slogan we find offensive, we

---

[3]Tversky, A., & Kahneman, D. (1974). Judgment under uncertainty: Heuristics and biases: Biases in judgments reveal some heuristics of thinking under uncertainty. *Science, 185*(4157), 1124–1131.

may make inferences about that person's intelligence, background, socio-economic status, and more.

But, first impressions are often wrong. They are also very hard to undo. We form a judgment about something and we often want to close the book on that judgment so we can create certainty and move on to other things.

This is particularly true for people who find decision-making taxing, such as when experiencing anxiety – something financial decision-making provokes in most of us. In those instances, we have an urgency to resolve issues – even at the expense of decision quality. Researchers refer to this as *need for cognitive closure*.[4] Many people have a low tolerance for uncertainty. And when tolerance is low, the pain or discomfort of decision-making is high. And what do we do when we're in pain? We figure out a way to stop the pain as soon as possible.

In such a scenario, a person will rush to find something – anything – to help move an issue from the "uncertain" or "undecided" column to the certain or decided column. And once something is decided, good luck getting that person to allow new information in that would force them to reconsider their position. To do so would be to invite that pain or discomfort back into their lives.

Psychologists Donna Webster and Arie Kruglanski refer to this as "seizing and freezing" where those high in a need for closure have an "urgency tendency" to reach a decision and a "permanence tendency" to resist reevaluating that decision.[5] This means that a person may refuse to consider new information that contradicts their initial evaluation. It also means that person is likely to actively avoid new information to avoid re-opening the decision-making process (and all the discomfort/pain that comes with it).

For many of us, certainty is preferable to accuracy. Since we may not admit to ourselves that we are likely sacrificing accuracy in our rush to judgment, we wear a shield of false-confidence regarding a decision. As research has shown, the higher the need for closure, the

---

[4]Webster, D. M., & Kruglanski, A. W. (1994). Individual differences in need for cognitive closure. *Journal of Personality and Social Psychology*, 67(6), 1049.

[5]Kruglanski, A. W., & Webster, D. M. (2018). Motivated closing of the mind: "Seizing" and "freezing". *The Motivated Mind*, 103(2), 60–103.

more confident – but less accurate – we tend to be in our decision-making.[6] Going forward, those high in the need for closure will also be less likely to admit – or attempt to correct – mistakes.

Bringing all of this back to the presentation of interest rates in loans, it means many of us will take the first rate as the true representation of the cost of the loan. We will anchor on that first presentation of a loan's cost and discount – if not completely avoid – the mandated presentation of a loan's true cost later in the process.

So, good effort TLA. We'll get 'em next time, I guess.

In all fairness, TLA did represent some progress. It has helped chip away at deceptive pricing practices in lending. Studies have shown TLA increased awareness and understanding of the price of debt – at least among higher income, higher education households.[7]

But, as we've already seen, higher income households have the least to fear when it comes to debt. As a percentage of household income, they hold less debt and at a better price than people of more modest means. They are also more likely to have been educated on some aspects of finance. Predatory lending, after all, thrives on inexperience and desperation to push high-interest debt on those least able to afford it.

Previously, interest could be described in just about any way lenders wanted. This provided multiple paths to obscuring costs.[8] Like discovering a pimple on your nose 10 minutes before a date, if lenders had an unappealing price on their product, they could simply try to cover it up. Instead of makeup to cover a zit, they used small print and even smaller loan terms to obscure the blemish of an exorbitant price.

Lenders would leave the unflattering price presentation out of their materials, and include a friendlier (often misleading) presentation. The end result was a variety of competing loans whose costs were being presented in a wide variety of ways. This prevented

[6]Stankov, L., & Crawford, J. D. (1997). Self-confidence and performance on tests of cognitive abilities. *Intelligence*, 25(2), 93–109.
[7]Durkin, T. A. (1981). Consumer awareness of installment credit terms: The impact of truth in lending after the passage of time. *Journal of Retail Banking*, 3(1), 21–32.
[8]Lee, J., & Hogarth, J. M. (1999). The price of money: Consumers' understanding of APRs and contract interest rates. *Journal of Public Policy & Marketing*, 18(1), 66–76.

consumers from being able to directly compare rates in the same terms. There would be no "apples-to-apples" comparison available to the borrower. It was comparing apples, oranges, car tires, and toaster ovens. As a result, the risk or expense of the loan would be underestimated by the consumer.

For example, there's the practice of "monthly rates." When you first hear the term "monthly rate" you may grow anxious at the notion of converting a monthly rate to an annual one, or vice versa. You may even assume that – given all the complexities of finance and compounding interest – it's impossible for someone without a graduate degree in finance to make such a conversion. How in the world can you pull off such an astounding quantitative feat? Take the annual rate and divide it by 12 to get the monthly rate. Or, take the monthly rate and multiply it by 12 to get the APR.

Simple. But only if you know how. And you wouldn't bother to convert the rate unless you had a sense that something was misleading. For many, anything related to interest rates is too intimidating to broach or attempt to analyze.

Why did TLA require lenders to put APRs on their loans? Because, how you present the price affects how people perceive the risk of their loans, particularly when people don't grasp the impact of compound interest. As we've discussed, those with the lowest knowledge base on a topic are the most easily persuadable.[9] In such a scenario, small marketing maneuvers have big impacts in terms of people's ability to understand (or misunderstand) the cost of something.

That credit card that charged you a sobering 18% APR? That's a monthly rate of 1.5%. And when you hear 1.5% monthly interest, that seems reasonable, perhaps even cheap. It's not.

Forcing all lenders to communicate interest rates in a common form (APR) was an important step. Such a thing helps consumers get a sense of relative expense of the product they're considering. But, laws like TLA don't prevent lenders from presenting interest rates in the most favorable light possible. It just requires that somewhere in the documentation, there needs to be an APR listed.

---

[9]Cialdini, R. B. (2006). *Influence: The psychology of persuasion* (Revised ed.). William Morrow.

Non-alignable Attributes

One key area of research that applies to this scenario is on *non-alignable attributes*. With any purchase, consumers are going to choose from at least two options. When doing that, they're going to look for a common basis of comparison between the two. Price, quality, and convenience are perhaps the most common high-level attributes to compare.

As a marketer, you obviously want to present a version of your product that is clearly superior to your competitor. Easy enough. But if your product is, in fact, *inferior* to the competition, then the path forward is not so obvious. The answer is to stimulate a basis of comparison on either:

- An attribute where you are superior.

- An attribute that the competition either doesn't have or isn't promoting.

- This is what is known as a non-alignable attribute. A consumer cannot compare this attribute directly to the competition.

For example, let's say you're caught in a love triangle. If you're being honest with yourself, you understand that your romantic rival is better-looking and more financially successful than you. But, based on the love interest's comments, it seems like you are more fun and thoughtful than your rival.

If the basis of your love interest's ultimate choice is either looks or money, you're likely to lose. Truth be told, your love interest *isn't sure* what the basis of his/her decision should be. Because of this, you have an opportunity to influence the basis of the decision. You need to emphasize how much more fun and/or thoughtful you are and how that is truly the foundation of a good relationship. If that becomes the criteria for the love interest's decision, you'll win.

Similarly, in the context of consumer credit, lenders have the freedom to not only emphasize their brand or product, but on what criteria consumers should base their decisions. And, as we've discussed, most people aren't sure how to evaluate loan products, so the lender will have an above-average opportunity to persuade the consumer.

Studies have shown that when comparing two similar products, the comparison of aligned attributes are more memorable and influential in consumer choice.[10] Let's look at an example in consumer lending – check-cashing services. While there are many reputable and well-intentioned lenders in consumer credit, check-cashing services are some of the most predatory lenders out there. They cater to the 25% of Americans who live in a household with little or no access to traditional banking services.[11]

This population is not going to a bank to cash a check or get a loan – there aren't any in their neighborhood. Instead, they are forced to seek out a financial services company in their area – typically predatory lender in the form of a check cashing retailer, car title lender, or pawn shop.

Lacking access to traditional banking services means you lack access to competitive prices and price transparency for loans. There are no mainstream lenders for this market and no competitive rates to be found. When 75% of Americans "shop around" for a short-term loan, they may be choosing between a 15% and 20% APR. When the remaining 25% of the country "shops around" for such a loan, they may be choosing between 150% and 200% or – in all likelihood – more.

This 25% of Americans without access to banking services are also disproportionately poor and of lower education. This lower level of education likely means a lack of sophistication and understanding as it relates to finance. Both unfortunately and unfairly, these factors make this population chum for predatory lenders.[12]

Let's look at advertising for Check Into Cash™, a large check-cashing retail business with over 1,000 locations in 30 states.

---

[10]Zhang, S., & Markman, A. B. (1998). Overcoming the early entrant advantage: The role of alignable and nonalignable differences. *Journal of Marketing Research*, *35*(4), 413–426.
[11]Barry, E. (2019, March 9). 25% of US Households are either unbanked or underbanked. *CNBC*. https://www.cnbc.com/2019/03/08/25percent-of-us-households-are-either-unbanked-or-underbanked.html. Accessed on October 5, 2022.
[12]For the non-fishers out there, chum is a mix of fish guts thrown into water by fishermen meant to attract predator fish like sharks.

If you look at their advertising, they primarily advertise their business on the attribute of convenience.[13] When it comes to pricing, they mention several times that the service is available for "just a flat fee." How convenient! A flat fee! And the people on the commercial were so excited about that fee, you have to assume that the fee is both snuggly and affordable. It is not. That convenience fee will eat your liver with a side of fava beans and a nice chianti.

Based on the fees buried several clicks into their website, Check Into Cash's fee for cashing a $100 check from you is $30.[14] A $200 check has a fee of $50. In your mind, you may rationalize that fee as "Meh. It's basically a stiff ATM fee," or "The fee is 25–30%."[15] You would be very wrong on both accounts!

You may also tell yourself that this is a one-off transaction. "It's expensive, but just this once." But for many, like eating that first potato chip in the bag, the first visit to a high-interest lender sets a financial cycle in motion that makes subsequent visits more and more likely.

When annualized, based on the *company's own calculations*, the APR of the fee for the $100 check is 782% and for the $200 check is 651%. That is the power of price presentation. When the interest rate is atrocious or even criminal (at least in some states), don't call it an interest rate. Call it something else.

Well, I could call baldness a "cosmetically care-free and more aerodynamic lifestyle" but I still have to own lots of hats and sunscreen. Putting a pleasant spin on something doesn't change its nature. Giving prices different names lowers the *perceived* risk of a loan but it doesn't change its *actual* risk.

In these instances, the best thing a borrower can do is ask for the APR of a loan and a disclosure of all fees. Lenders are required by law to provide them. Unfortunately, this will also require you to do the significant work of laying out all cost components and comparing them. But the amount you will save will be profound.

---

[13]For example: https://www.youtube.com/watch?v=hMfqKJRXFAs.
[14]https://checkintocash.com/wp-content/uploads/LA-Fee-Schedule-090117.pdf. Accessed on October 5, 2022.
[15]If you convert ATM fees to an APR, they are shockingly expensive rates – ON YOUR OWN MONEY! You're not even borrowing it! Yet, if you pay $3 to withdraw $100 every week, that's a weekly interest rate of 3% times 52 weeks. Your APR is over 150%.

WHAT CAN YOU DO?

You better shop around. – Smokey Robinson[16]

The good news is that you can defeat a lender's attempt to obscure pricing. The bad news is that it takes significant effort to do it. You have to do the work to find all the prices and fees. Then you have to do the math to figure out the total cost. Lastly, you should look at a competitive loan offering and do that same work. If the thought of doing all that work makes you anxious or sleepy, you're not alone. But it will be very much worth your while if you do.

We have a tendency to think that loan offers are the result of some mystical formula based solely on our credit rating. But the truth is there is a wide discrepancy both in the rates offered and those accepted by customers, regardless of credit score.

Consider the work of two Economics professors – Victor Stango and Jonathan Zinman. Besides sounding like two cops in a movie that get results by not playing by the rules – they have examined thousands of consumer loans to understand what affects the price people pay for credit. And while we are conditioned to think that the answer is credit score, what they found will surprise you.

Credit scores do affect the price you pay for credit. But, it's not the biggest factor. The biggest factor is how much effort you put into finding the best deal. Controlling for credit scores, the difference in shopping effort of borrowers accounted for the biggest differences in prices paid. Let's say you have two people with the same credit scores, and one searched extensively for the best deal on a credit card, while the other didn't. The difference in the interest rates paid by those people would likely equal the difference between the rate given to someone with the highest possible credit score versus another with the lowest.[17] In other words, you can lower the cost of your loans as much or more by shopping around and

---

[16]The song "Shop Around" by The Miracles (Smokey's first band). Copyright 1960, Motown Records.
[17]Stango, V., & Zinman, J. (2016). Borrowing high versus borrowing higher: price dispersion and shopping behavior in the US credit card market. *The Review of Financial Studies*, 29(4), 979–1006.

reading the fine print as you can by maintaining a high credit score. The authors refer to this as "search intensity."

Stango and Zinman estimate that US credit card holders are paying $45 billion more in interest *per year* than they would if they had made more of an effort.[18] If anything, these numbers appear to be low as the researchers' sample skewed toward higher income, higher education card holders who were likely to get better deals.

So, the lesson is clear: instead of jumping on the first loan offer to reduce your discomfort and anxiety, shop around. A lot. It will, 99 times out 100, save you significant money. And if you're not sure what to do – and most of us aren't – get help. From a friend, a non-profit or somewhere else.

---

[18]It was estimated at $36 Billion in 2016, when the study was published. I adjusted the number for inflation for 2023 numbers.

10

DEALING WITH MULTIPLE PRICE COMPONENTS

SIMPLICITY IN MARKETING

Those who study and practice marketing will tell you that simplicity is one of the primary goals of an advertisement. Simplicity functions as a spotlight that highlights a key benefit about your product to a potential customer. It increases something academics refer to as "processing fluency" – the ease and speed with which we understand something.[1]

The simpler the message, the more fluently we process it. A thoughtfully simple message commands the audience's attention, is instantly understood, and long remembered. Our fluent processing of that message will also cause us to perceive the product more positively. Then, when a prospective customer is contemplating a purchase, he/she will be:

- more likely to recall that product;

- more motivated to seek it out; and

- more inclined to make the purchase.

---

[1] Song, H., & Schwarz, N. (2008). If it's hard to read, it's hard to do: Processing fluency affects effort prediction and motivation. *Psychological Science*, *19*(10), 986–988.

When done well, the combination of a simple message highlighting a valued benefit can enable that message to live on in our minds. Here are a few classic examples (Table 3).

Table 3. Famous Corporate Slogans Communicating a Benefit.

Company	Message	Benefit Conveyed
Allstate insurance	"You're in good hands with Allstate."	Trustworthiness – we're not going to hang you out to dry on a claim.
Enterprise Rent-a-Car	"At enterprise, we'll pick you up."	Easiest rental car experience.
Snicker's	"Hungry? Snap into a Snickers."	The most filling candy bar available for when you can't get to a meal.
Burger King	"Have it your way."	Service. We're not going to freak out if you ask us to not put pickles on your cheeseburger.

BUT… COMPLEXITY HAS ITS PLACE TOO (UNFORTUNATELY)

If simplicity is the key to *increasing* attention, comprehension, and memory, then complexity is the key to *decreasing* it.

One of my favorite headlines from the satirical website *The Onion* reads: "Nation shudders at large block of uninterrupted text."[2] We all know that feeling – the dread we get when looking at something that looks confusing and/or complex. It is instantly de-motivating. We can feel our energy reserves drain out of us when we see large blocks of text anywhere. Text books. Instruction manuals. Fine print.

And if you're like me, a lot of times the intimidation can result in you ignoring the information all together. You forgo the instruction

---

[2]The Onion. (2010, March 9). Nation shudders at large block of uninterrupted text. *The Onion*. https://www.theonion.com/nation-shudders-at-large-block-of-uninterrupted-text-1819571366. Accessed on December 5, 2022.

manual and think, "I know how this works." Or, "I can figure this out." And then, the bed frame from Ikea™ you're attempting to assemble has a dozen leftover pieces when you're done and everyone in the house is too scared to sleep on it. (And they're right to be!)

Think of complexity in communication as "attention repellant" to readers. It discourages and de-motivates us. Complexity makes us less likely to read, understand, or remember something. For those reasons, if you're a marketer attempting to educate the public about a key product benefit, you avoid complexity and strive for simplicity.

But there are instances when a marketer would want to decrease a consumer's attention, comprehension, and memory about a product. And that's when talking about the product's *costs*.

As mentioned earlier, debt is a product category that competes almost exclusively on the basis of cost. This incentivizes some lenders to create the *appearance* of being less expensive than it actually is. And this is achieved through complexity. What is the key way of introducing complexity to your pricing? By:

- Having multiple price components for your debt.

- Not acknowledging all of the pricing components as prices (calling them late fees, convenience fees, points, processing charges, etc.).

- Not putting pricing components next to each other, but spreading cost information throughout sales materials or loan disclosures.

By doing this, marketers can take advantage of consumers' over-taxed attention spans as well as their general anxiety about anything involving money and/or math.

BEYOND INTEREST

Earlier in this book, we saw that interest rates provide a unique set of challenges to consumers. And, if interest rates were all we had to understand about debt, we'd still have our work cut out for us. But most debt products come with a lot more prices than just an interest rate.

This is particularly true for mortgages, where there are late fees, closing fees, realtor commissions, inspection fees, mortgage insurance, mortgage points, and more. Being able to accurately assess the total cost of something becomes virtually impossible. And you get so fatigued and delirious from the complexity of the purchase, you might be willing to pay almost anything to be done with the process.

What happens when there are multiple prices that must be paid in order to acquire the desired product? Or, to further complicate things, what happens when not all prices are identified as prices? Lastly, are people able to understand the ramifications of prices that change (usually for the worse!) over the use of that product?

MEET MULTI-COMPONENT, OR "PARTITIONED" PRICING

Likely the most common form of multi-component pricing we see is when ordering something online. There is the price for the product you pay, and then there is some price to get the product shipped to you.[3]

Let's say you are buying shoes online and the price for the shoes is $50 plus $7 shipping. You have also looked at those same shoes at a store in the mall. Those are available for $55 with no shipping charge. Some consumers will compare those options and arrive at the conclusion that the online shoes are cheaper. After all, the "price" ($50 vs. $55) is five dollars cheaper, even if the total cost to the buyer ($57 vs. $55) is not.

And this simple, low-stakes example gives you a key insight into partitioned prices. When you have prices that are set apart and given different names – shipping, handling, account maintenance, activation fee, etc. – it dramatically increases the level of difficulty in understanding, remembering, and comparing prices. It also takes people's focus off the total cost of the transaction.

Typically, *we remember or process one price for a good* – even if that good actually has multiple price components. The more

---

[3]Yes, Amazon Prime™ customers, I see you. You don't pay "shipping." You pay X dollars a year to get "free" shipping. Totally different eye roll.

components of a price there are, the less likely a customer will be able to accurately process the total cost of a good.

In the shoe example, we understand the "price" as one thing ($50 vs. $55). We may not even contemplate "total cost" ($57 vs. $55). That is likely because the number labeled "price" gets most of our attention and focus – known as the "focal price." And that focal price becomes deeply imprinted on our brain while "shipping" goes into some waste bin in our mind.

Partitioned pricing is the practice of promoting the focal price for a product while deemphasizing the other costs/prices associated with that good. You see marketers promote focal prices all the time in a variety of contexts. Perhaps most commonly, you see focal pricing in grocery stores. Your favorite grocer will advertise sale prices on the goods to which you pay the most attention. Seeing a discount on products you care about often will get you more motivated to go to that store.

If you love junk food like me, that means ice cream. The market down the street will advertise half-priced pints of Ben & Jerry's knowing that I will race to the store squealing with glee the whole way. And once I'm at the store? That grocer also knows I'll pick up other, non-discounted (or even inflated!) goods while at the store. Then, I will brag to my friends and family about being a smart shopper that only paid $3 for a pint of Chunky Monkey™, even though I also paid $25 for a bag of carrots in that same trip.

Partitioned pricing is, in many ways, the classic misdirection of a magic trick. Use a distraction to take the audience's attention away from a manipulation in order to create a misperception. For a magician, the manipulation is having a rabbit stuffed in the sleeve of his/her jacket. The distraction is having a scantily clad assistant walk on to stage at the moment the magician slips the rabbit into the hat. This creates the misperception that something mystical or supernatural has happened when the audience later notices the rabbit is sitting in the hat. But, nothing magical has happened. You were just paying attention to the wrong thing.

For sellers practicing "dark pricing magic," it's a similar process. The manipulation is partitioning the prices. The distraction is calling attention to the focal price while reducing attention to other price components, often by calling them by different names such as "shipping and handling," "convenience fee," and so on. The buyer then considers only the focal price instead of the total cost to acquire the item. This creates the misperception that the cost of the product is lower than it actually is and... Ta da! You got overcharged!

For the record, partitioning prices is not *always* about shaking down the consumer for a few extra bucks. Sometimes, such as with cell phone service, the purpose is to let consumers know which fees are going to the provider and which are the result of outside costs like taxes.

But often times, the purpose of partitioned pricing *is* to confuse people and make the total cost less obvious.[4] And partitioned pricing is on the rise. Why? It's the same reason that other universally despised marketing tools like SPAM email and robocalling continue to be used. It's cheap to implement and it works! After much price experimentation and resulting sales data, companies know for a fact that the shell game of partitioned pricing makes them significantly more money at little-to-no extra expense.

And, consumers are usually none the wiser. In fact, they often *prefer* partitioned prices, even though it's to their economic detriment. Research has shown that consumers find partitioned pricing persuasive and informative.[5] They feel that they are getting a better sense of the costs being incurred by the seller. In the consumer's mind, that helps justify the expense.

Like with anything misleading, there is a kernel of truth to that rationale. Consumers are pretty fair-minded as a group. In general, they don't mind absorbing extra expense if they feel that same expense has been paid by the seller. The difference is that the "expense" that gets partitioned is often a pre-existing, standard cost of doing business. And, partitioning those prices is often done with the intent of making an ordinary expense seem unusual so the consumer will not be bothered by paying extra for it.

---

[4]Greenleaf, E. A., Johnson, E. J., Morwitz, V. G., & Shalev, E. (2016). The price does not include additional taxes, fees, and surcharges: A review of research on partitioned pricing. *Journal of Consumer Psychology*, 26(1), 105–124.
[5]Kim, H. M. (2006). The effect of salience on mental accounting: how integration versus segregation of payment influences purchase decisions. *Journal of Behavioral Decision Making*, 19(4), 381–391.

HOW WE DECIDE IF WE'LL TOLERATE A FEE

Context is vitally important in our deciding which additional fees we will or will not accept. We get conditioned over time about accepting or rejecting certain pricing practices. If a fee seems common for a context or class of product, we learn to accept it.

Growing up, the notion of a "delivery fee" for a pizza was offensive. Domino's and other pizza delivery chains continuously advertised "free delivery." This, despite the fact it should have been obvious they were just rolling delivery costs into their prices. As someone who delivered pizzas all through college, I can tell you that when these companies would occasionally experiment with a separate delivery fee, the customer backlash was immediate and harsh. Consumers came to learn delivery as something that was included in the price of the pizza.

Ironically, consumers did not appear to make the connection between delivery fees and "take out discounts" – lower prices for people who came to the store to pick up their pizzas. It seemed reasonable to consumers that you would pay less if the pizza place did not have to send a driver. Implicitly, this meant customers understood there was cost to getting a pizza delivered.

Consumers were comfortable with take-out discounts. But, if you explicitly charged them for delivery? Those of us taking orders at the pizza place would hear a stream of obscenities from customers. It was a silly, illogical distinction. But, the pizza companies had to adapt and play the game, at least until consumer sentiment could be changed.

Over time, the popularity of services like GrubHub™ have normalized delivery fees. Why? A fee from a third-party service that focuses only on delivery seemed like a different animal than that same fee from the maker of the food. After repeated interactions with delivery fees, consumers began to accept the notion of delivery fees in general.

Let's go back to the example of buying shoes. Wasn't the store in the mall also incurring shipping expense to get those shoes out to their showroom? But if the store in the mall put "plus shipping" next to the price of Nikes that are right in front of you, the consumer is going to feel cheated and cry foul. The context is off.

In the consumer's experience, stores in the mall do not charge for shipping. That's something that only online providers do.

Plus, in the consumer's mind, those shoes were not being shipped. "Shipping," in the consumer's mind, means having the product brought to his/her door. But the pair of Nikes in the store *was* shipped. Those shoes traveled 8,000 miles from China to the store's distribution center somewhere in the United States. Then, a truck carried the shoes across the country to the store that's a quarter-mile from your house. But, that type of shipping exists outside the costumer's understanding and will not be tolerated as an additional expense. So, the store rolls that cost into final price to avoid irritating the consumer.

Anecdotally, we are familiar with running into partitioned prices and surcharges in a variety of other contexts as well. If you're looking to rent an AirBnB™, you may notice that some places have a very low nightly rate, but an extremely high "cleaning fee." Those high cleaning fee property owners are playing with partitioned pricing to boost revenue.

They give you a low focal price (nightly rate) and a high surcharge or partitioned price (cleaning fee). AirBnB also gives the property owner an assist by not displaying cleaning fees in the initial listing for the property to direct more attention to the focal price ("nightly rate") and away from the total cost.[6] Requiring you to click or drill down on a property to see all the expenses is a way of creating additional distance between the focal price and the other price components.

It's pretty silly, actually. Since we have started using AirBnB, we have had to deal with cleaning fees. They are now standard. As a result, we accept them as they are familiar to us in that context. Yet, in every other context of short-term room or housing rentals, we expect cleaning to be included in the nightly rate. Hey AirBnB, why stop at cleaning fees? Why not have a mortgage fee, "building not collapsing" fee, locking door fee, bed fee, no rodent fee, and others?

If a hotel attempted to charge us a cleaning fee for a room, we'd lose our minds with righteous anger. Hotels have not traditionally

---

[6]AirBnB – to their credit – has since made presentation of total cost an option for customers.

charged an explicit fee for that. In both contexts, we have an expectation of renting a room that is clean. But, only in one context do we accept that there is an associated cost. This is as we accept shipping fees from online sellers of goods and not stores in the mall.

WE SEEM TO PREFER DECEPTIVE PRICING

Human beings are pretty easy marks when it comes to deceptive pricing. We actually seem to *like* being deceived in this way. Behavioral research tells us so.

Consumers have a demonstrated *preference* for partitioned pricing even though it costs them more. We report a greater intent to buy when encountering partitioned prices than when given a single, "all-in" price.[7] For instance, one study found that bidders for items on eBay do not take shipping fees (which are set by the seller) into account.[8] People bid the same for two identical items, even if one of the items hits you with a significantly higher shipping cost after you win the bid. Another study found that stores who include sales tax in their list prices experience lower demand versus when they add tax at checkout.[9]

Outside of the laboratory, there are many real-world examples of consumers preferring, even demanding, more complex pricing. Ticket service StubHub™ stopped partitioning its prices and made tickets available at a single, "all-in" price. The result? Customers bought fewer tickets.[10] JC Penny got rid of flashy sales promotions

---

[7]Morwitz, V. G., Greenleaf, E. A., & Johnson, E. J. (1998). Divide and prosper: Consumers' reactions to partitioned prices. *Journal of Marketing Research*, 35(4), 453–463.
[8]Hossain, T., & Morgan, J. (2006). plus shipping and handling: Revenue (non) equivalence in field experiments on ebay. *The BE Journal of Economic Analysis & Policy*, 6(2), 27.
[9]Chetty, R., Looney, A., & Kroft, K. (2009). Salience and taxation: Theory and evidence. *American Economic Review*, 99(4), 1145–1177.
[10]Karp, H. (2014, March). StubHub sings the blues after shifting fees: Attempt at price transparency backfires, hurting sales. *The Wall Street Journal*, 26. https://www.wsj.com/articles/stubhub-sings-the-blues-after-shifting-fees-1395783228

(normally $100, now 20% off for a short time only) in favor of "always low prices." The result? A drop in sales.[11]

While we, as consumers, bemoan the use of confusing or misleading prices, the truth is we bear at least part of the blame. Often times, we are in too much of a rush, or feel too put upon to do the necessary work of determining the true costs of things. As a result, we pay more than we should.

PARTITIONED PRICING IN DEBT

In the shoe example we are talking about a potential miscalculation of $2. In the AirBnB example, we're talking about 50 or a 100 dollars. When it comes to debt products like mortgages, these miscalculations can cost us hundreds or thousands of dollars. Here are just a few of the common add-on fees associated with loans:

- Document fees: The cost to process the paperwork associated with the loan.

- Disbursement fees: The cost to actually disburse the money agreed to in the loan (most common in student loans).

- Origination fees: The cost to establish the loan.

- Prepayment penalties: A fee for paying off your loan ahead of time.

- Application fees: The cost for getting the lender to consider lending you money.

- Late payment fees.

- Credit insurance fees: The cost of insuring the loan if the applicants credit rating is not optimal or not enough of a down payment has been offered (most common in mortgages).

---

[11]D'innocenzio, A. (2012, January 25). JC Penny gets rid of hundreds of sales. *The Seattle Times*. https://www.seattletimes.com/business/jc-penney-gets-rid-of-hundreds-of-sales/. Accessed on November 14, 2022.

Our ability to recognize these partitioned prices and account for them in the total cost will vary based on a variety of things. These include how prominently and clearly the add-on cost is presented or how motivated we are to assess all the costs.

WHAT CAN BORROWERS DO?

So much of assessing the actual cost of a loan involves getting over the anxiety of evaluating loans. We have angst about finance because it's very important and have the sneaking (and usually correct) suspicion that we don't fully understand what we're getting ourselves into.

Key to getting the best deal on a loan and understanding its true cost involves:

- *Taking a deep breath* and understanding that almost everyone feels the way you do.

- *Don't runaway from the discomfort, run toward it.* The best way to get comfortable with something is to embrace it and have repeated exposures to it.

- *Do the work of understanding the true cost.* Find the mandated "truth in lending" disclosure that is required in all consumer loan products in the US. If you don't see it, ask the lender for it. This will get you an "at a glance" view of all the costs of the loan. It will also provide an "apples-to-apples" basis of comparison for other loan offers, which brings us to...

- *Get multiple offers for a loan.* Remember, the price of a loan is less determined by a person's credit score than by how much they shopped around.

11

DRIP PRICING

I was too weak to give in. Too strong to lose...Is someone getting the best of you?[1] – Foo Fighters

Much of this book is about things that make it hard to a make a good initial decision. This chapter is about our common inability to acknowledge and correct a bad decision. Metaphorically speaking, as our car barrels toward the edge of a cliff, human nature is not to hit the brakes. Often, it's to hit the accelerator.

THE DRIP, DRIP, DRIP OF PARTITIONED PRICES

To recap, the probability of paying more than we should or realize, goes up with:

- the number of separate or "partitioned" prices attached to a good (how many);

- the number of different labels/names we attach to these price components (who or what);

- the number of different places in which these prices are located (where);

---

[1]Grohl, H., & Mendel, S. (2005). *Best of you [Recorded by Foo Fighters]*. On the album In Your Honor. RCA Records.

But there is another factor at play: *when* various pricing components are revealed to the customer. Price components that are displayed after the consumer has encountered the focal price have a lesser chance of being noticed, processed or remembered by the consumer.

This practice is called "drip pricing" – the slow reveal of costs to the consumer over the purchasing process. It is your basic "bait and switch": Lure the customer into committing to a product with an attractive price and then later reveal additional components of cost. As new prices for the product are revealed, the customer is often either resigned or oblivious to accepting the additional cost.

Drip pricing is perhaps most commonly seen in the purchase of airline tickets. Air travel is expensive. To minimize costs, you diligently scour the Internet looking for the best airfare. Eventually, you find the best balance of airfare and itinerary taking you out of the best airports, on the best days and times, and at the best price. You commit and click the button to purchase. What you are then subjected to is a cascade of options and fees. Baggage fees. Seat selection. Priority boarding. Ticketing fees. Travel insurance. And on. And on. And on.

Most consumers know these add-ons are coming after selecting the airfare. Yet, we fail to take them into account in our initial selection of a flight. There are so many add-ons and at such a wide variety of pricing. For example, a quick perusal of baggage fees by airline shows that a passenger will pay anywhere from $0–$225 for a bag *each way* of a trip.[2] Plus, different airlines have different standards for what constitutes a regular bag, an oversized bag, a carry-on, and so on. If you can remember the specific fees and policies for each airline then you officially have a super power, because that's something 99% of us cannot do.

Chances are you choose the flight you want and then just accept whatever comes next. These add-on prices are not revealed until far into the purchasing process after a traveler has made the herculean effort to find and *commit* to a flight with the best mix of times, dates, airports, and fares.

All of these options and fees obliterate whatever sense of value you thought you had determined for the flight when finding the initial fare. And, you were so focused on the "airfare" that you

---

[2]https://www.tripadvisor.com/AirlineFees. Accessed on December 22, 2022.

forget each airline has a unique array of options and fees that make it very difficult to anticipate (on the front end) or remember (on the back end) the total cost for the flight.

And these fees and options mean BIG BUCKS to the airlines. For example, European discount airline Ryan Air – the only airline that releases these figures – makes 1/3 of its revenues off of these fees.[3] Their philosophy appears to be getting people in with lower fares and then making their money on extra services (for luxury upgrades like….examines airline ticket….knowing where you're going to sit.). In 2017, these fees generated $57 billion for airlines in the US and $88 billion worldwide.[4]

Researchers recently found that when consumers shop for airline tickets, they predictably choose the lower "up front" stated price – the airfare before the additional fees.[5] No surprise there.

But what was surprising was when researchers manipulated the fees incurred after committing to the initial fare. The researchers made it so these "cheap" fares had highest total cost due to the extra fees. To exclude the possibility that participants perhaps just couldn't process the total cost, the researchers showed them that they paid a higher total cost than other options and offered the chance to switch. Participants refused. Why? There were a few reasons.

First, despite reporting a general feeling of getting screwed by all these fees, consumers did not want to invest the significant time and energy in going through the process again. At a certain point, people just want to move on.

Second, they understandably (though incorrectly) assumed that the lower total cost option was going cost just as much, if not more. This, despite the fact that they were shown otherwise. In other words, they were so mesmerized by all price components, the participants were resigned to getting deceived.

----

[3]Ciesluk, K. (2020, June 14). How do low cost carriers actually make money: A complete breakdown. *Simple Flying*. https://simpleflying.com/how-low-cost-carriers-make-money/. Accessed on September 8, 2022.
[4]Josephs, L. (2017, November 27). Airlines to rake in record $57 billion in passenger fees this year, study shows. *CNBC*. https://www.cnbc.com/2017/11/27/airlines-to-rake-in-record-57-billion-in-passenger-fees-this-year.html
[5]Santana, S., Dallas, S. K., & Morwitz, V. G. (2020). Consumer reactions to drip pricing. *Marketing Science*, 39(1), 188–210.

These first two reasons are pretty relatable. Shopping for airfares *is* exhausting. Having to repeat the process sounds as pleasant as dental surgery. Also, it's easy to become cynical about airfare pricing and the inevitability of an airline pulling the wool over your eyes. In fact, you could argue that consumer resignation about getting jammed on airfares is not the result of cynicism, but experience.

But the last reason found for consumer resistance to switching is perhaps the most instructive – people didn't want to admit they had made a mistake. After all, who likes admitting their mistakes?

Even though we constantly make mistakes, human nature is to deny having done so. And the bigger the mistake, the stronger the urge to deny having made it. How did the researchers know that this was the reason? Participants in the study, after being shown irrefutable evidence that they chose a bad deal, insisted they got a good one. In this instance, consumers weren't as concerned with saving time or money as they were with saving face. There was a psychological cost to admitting the error. So, they merely bent reality to save them from having to pay that psychological cost. They engaged in *self-justification*.

As its name suggests, self-justification is the practice of manipulating your reality to avoid a negative impact on your own self-image. Research on self-justification has shown when someone else makes a mistake, we are quick to point it out and correct it.[6]

But when *we* make the mistake? Not only do we *not* acknowledge it but we also tend to double-down. Our commitment to the bad decision escalates. And as our commitment to the bad decision escalates, we become less and less likely to correct course, regardless of new information we encounter. In the study I just mentioned, people who were shown that they had made a bad investment decision refused to acknowledge it. In fact, the worse their error, the more likely they were to allocate more funds to that bad investment. They didn't correct. They doubled-down.

---

[6]Staw, B. M. (1976). Knee-deep in the big muddy: A study of escalating commitment to a chosen course of action. *Organizational Behavior and Human Performance*, 16(1), 27–44.

Rather than deal with the embarrassment and confusion of having made a dopey decision, we tend to justify our actions. We see it all the time in various parts of our lives. If you root for the New York Yankees and see a Boston Red Sox player break the rules? You are likely to think such outrageous behavior is typical for your hated rival.

But if you see a member of your beloved Yankees do the same thing? Chances are you're likely to laugh it off or even express admiration for that player's "win at all costs" mentality. You make this distinction because you have invested a lot of yourself and your identity in rooting for that team. Your team cheating not only reflects badly on the team but it also reflects badly on you. You can either admit you root for a team that breaks the rules or you can change your view of rule-breaking. More often than not, you justify your rooting for that team by minimizing or even praising the controversial behavior.

To recap:

- Consumers have a frustrating experience buying plane tickets and pay more than they expect.

- They are shown a lower "total cost" option.

- They stick with the more expensive and frustrating option due to perceived monetary, nonmonetary (time, energy) and psychological (pride, self-image) costs associated with switching.

Now, let's look at how this applies to debt.

Drippy Loans

Air travel is perhaps the most notorious venue for drip pricing. But it is every bit as common in personal finance. Credit cards, mortgages, and other forms of debt usually feature pricing components that reveal themselves after the initial point of purchase.

The most dramatic example of drip pricing related to debt is in mortgages. And if you thought airlines could get you to accept a mountain of fees in the five minutes it takes to buy a ticket, just wait until you spend a month and a half going through the process of purchasing a home.

From the moment a seller accepts an offer from a buyer, the process of "closing" that purchase is typically 30–45 days. In that time, the buyer must finalize the terms of the mortgage. The buyer must also meet the lender's stipulations for getting the house inspected, insured, assessed for value, current on taxes, and more. And that "truth in lending" disclosure that's going to summarize all your costs for you? You're only going to get a final version of that once you've satisfied all of those stipulations. Plus, depending on how things like inspections and assessments go, it could cause your lender to change the terms of the loan from what was originally discussed.

When you add the [extraordinary] amount of time and effort required to find a house you want and negotiate a price, there is a considerable amount of commitment to that purchase. To walk away from a mortgage provider is to risk not being able to close on that house. And to risk that is to invite the possibility of:

• Not being able to close on that home.

• Not having a place to live.

• Having to repeat the search and purchase process for a different home (Dear God).

Because of this, any significant changes to the cost of the home or the terms of the loan are highly likely to be tolerated. Same with any new fees or expenses late in the process. A buyer in the middle of a home purchase is <u>highly</u> committed to closing.

When a buyer is limited in his/her ability or inclination to walk away, that person is surrendering A LOT of power in the process. If you are dealing with an ethically challenged banker or mortgage broker, you may find that deep into the purchase process:

• Your interest rate is higher than initially promised.

• New expenses like mortgage insurance may be introduced.

• Terms of the loan may change to include things like pre-payment penalties.

These are some of the most common types of unsavory tactics. A couple of days before closing on a house, borrowers may get a call from their mortgage broker saying, "There was a problem. . ." where the terms of the loan have to change. And the terms of the loan can result in a monthly mortgage payment that could be about 30% higher (or more) than originally thought.

As with exorbitant baggage fees for an airline ticket, your commitment to the purchase is likely to cost you significantly more money.

OTHER SOURCES OF DRIP ON A MORTGAGE

Once you begin the closing process, you begin the process of figuring out what the purchase is actually going to cost. You receive something called the "HUD1" form – a three-page form that is designed to provide an easy "at-a-glance" summary of all potential fees and charges related to buying a house. And when you see this form, your head is likely to swoon. Here are all the potential prices/fees covered in the form.

- Contract sales price.

- Settlement charges.

- City taxes.

- County taxes.

- Sales fees/commissions.

- Appraisal fee.

- Credit report fee.

- Flood certification.

- Mortgage insurance.

- Property taxes.

- Property insurance.

- Title fee.

- Title insurance.

- Government recording charges.

- City/County/State "Stamps".

- Loan origination charge.

- Loan interest rate.

- Loan "points".

- Loan late payment penalties.

- Loan early payment penalties.

- Loan balloon payment(s).

This is from the form that was designed to make a home purchase easier and *more* transparent. The only thing transparent here is that this house is going to cost you a lot more than you originally thought.

And, sadly enough, it *IS* an improvement over prior loan documentation.

Consumer advocates and government agencies work hard to make sure that home buyers know what they're getting into in terms of the real month-to-month expense of purchasing and owning a home. But with so many fees and prices associated with the transaction, it's very difficult to produce a completely transparent transaction.

Plus, while some of these fees and prices are pretty-straight forward, like $35 for a credit check, many aren't. Points on a mortgage, for instance, are complex and confusing. Here's a very quick primer for those unfamiliar with points on a mortgage. In attempting to get a better overall price (read: interest rate) on a mortgage, borrowers often have the option of paying a fee to lower the interest rate. That can sound good. However, the merit of paying points on a loan depends on the price of the points, and the length and amount of the mortgage. And those merits will vary depending on your age, career prospects, and appreciation of the house. It's like doubling all of the factors that made the original cost of a mortgage difficult to understand.

WHAT CONSUMERS CAN DO TO RESIST THE
GRAVITATIONAL PULL OF DRIP PRICING

- Be willing to walk away (you often find the lender will mirac-
ulously come up with a better offer).

- Do the math.

- If you are a man partnered with a woman, solicit your partner's
input! This is not only good for harmony and equity in the relationship, studies have shown that women are less prone to escalating commitment in financial decision-making than men.[7] It is
evocative of the cliché of men being too stubborn to ask directions
when they're clearly lost. This applies to financial decision-making
as well. Men, swallow your pride and ask directions.

In most of these chapters, I recommend "taking a deep breath" or
some other stress-relieving activity. Anxiety is generally problematic
in decision-making. It narrows our views. Stress often makes us
focused on either the wrong things or too few of them. It makes it
harder to perceive the proverbial forest for the trees.

When it comes to escalating commitment, however, it sometimes
has its place. Those in drip pricing or other scenarios prone to
escalating commitment are often likely to walk away when they
experience negative emotions such as anxiety.[8] Many seek an
"avoidance" strategy of just wanting to be done with the situation
without having to decide. And in the case of drip pricing, if the
subsequent prices revealed later in the deal truly change the nature
or fairness of it, that can be a good thing.

---

[7]Bateman, T. S. (1986). The escalation of commitment in sequential decision
making: Situational and personal moderators and limiting conditions.
Decision Sciences, 17(1), 33–49.
[8]Endler, N. S., & Parker, J. D. (1990). Multidimensional assessment of
coping: A critical evaluation. *Journal of Personality and Social Psychology*,
58(5), 844.

12

CREDIT CARD REWARDS

On a basic level, rewards programs are designed to incentivize loyalty to a particular brand. Whether it's punch cards for a free coffee or miles for free flights, we are all familiar with the basic goal and structure of rewards programs. A purveyor of something wants to compel you to make repeat purchases and not stray to a competitor. They offer you some benefit contingent upon making repeat purchases. And, when you might be tempted to stray from this vendor, the vendor hopes the loyalty program is compelling enough to make you hesitate for a moment and say, "Only two more visits for a free sandwich." And back to Subway™ you'll go – even if that's not what you were really in the mood for.

The overall value proposition is *extremely* lopsided. You may not want to eat 10 chili dogs in the next month to get a free sundae at Dairy Queen™. But, you make the considered decision that you're going to go for it, and you'll feel like a champion when you're holding that frosty reward.

The success of loyalty programs, combined with the advent of technologies like mobile applications making them easier to implement, have made them a necessity for retailers. They are *everywhere*. In fact, we are drowning in them.

On average, each US household belongs to 16.6 loyalty pro-grams.[1] It's why our wallets are overstuffed with punch cards, our keychains are crowded with scan tags, and our phones are littered with retail apps. It raises the question: If *everyone* has a loyalty program and we belong to most (if not all) of them, is it really keeping us loyal?

Yes! Every time we get pitched by a cashier, flight attendant, or TV commercial to sign up for a new rewards program, we think to ourselves, "Do I need another app/card/tag and all the e-mail SPAM that results from it?" We think that, but ultimately, we relent and sign up.

The truth is... We *love* rewards! And we don't just respond to them as incentives, research has shown we *over*-respond to them.[2] Anecdotally, you've seen it where people line up and wait hours for a free ice cream cone at *Ben & Jerry's* that would have cost them $4. If time is money – and it is – then there's really no rational explanation for committing that kind of time and energy for such a small reward. But then again, it *is* fun. It *does* make us feel good. And those feelings are why we love rewards and incentives.

In fact, we love them so much they have a profound effect on our purchasing behavior. In the game of life, there aren't that many prizes – especially once you reach adulthood. And rewards pro-grams give us prizes! The potential for prizes not only makes us consider a repeat purchase but it can make us ignore cheaper, higher quality, or more convenient options. They even contribute to our sense of identity and social status.[3] Sounds ridiculous? It is! But this is human behavior we're talking about.

Researchers have looked at the effect of rewards programs on purchasing behaviors. Not only do they affect our choice to revisit a retailer or brand, we conjure reasons to do so more often. Consider

──────────
[1]Statista. (2022). Average loyalty program membership in the United States from 2015 to 2021. https://www.statista.com/statistics/618744/average-number-of-loyalty-programs-us-consumers-belong-to/. Accessed on October 17, 2022.
[2]Shampanier, K., Mazar, N., & Ariely, D. (2007). Zero as a special price: The true value of free products. *Marketing Science*, 26(6), 742–757.
[3]Dreze, X., & Nunes, J. C. (2009). Feeling superior: The impact of loyalty program structure on consumers' perceptions of status. *Journal of Consumer Research*, 35(6), 890–905.

one study that examined data from a coffee punch card program that required the purchase of 10 coffees to get the 11th free. It found that loyalty program accelerated customer purchases the closer they got to reaching their reward.[4] Similar effects were found on airline miles.[5] We change our purchasing decisions based on potential rewards. And, often times, we don't realize we're doing it.

This effect is in keeping with research on goal attainment. The closer we get to accomplishing a goal, the more we intensify our pursuit.[6] But goals come in all shapes and sizes.

Sure, as a child, you dreamed of becoming an astronaut. That was quite an impressive goal! Now, you're trying to get a free coffee. Well... that's a goal, too (though your mother may be less likely to brag to her friends about it). And, as you get closer to your free coffee with a punch card or free flight with a miles program, you try harder to make that happen. You purchase more often than you would have otherwise.

CREDIT CARD INCENTIVES – MILE AFTER MILE OF MENTAL ACCOUNTING MISTAKES

As discussed in mental accounting, categorizing our expenses and income, and dealing with them in a consistent manner is tricky. We may label some things in our mind as "free" when they clearly are not. This is especially the case with credit card rewards. These incentives come in two forms, most commonly:

- *Cash Back:* Where the credit card holder receives a rebate, typically at the rate of 1%.

---

[4]Kivetz, R., Urminsky, O., & Zheng, Y. (2006). The goal-gradient hypothesis resurrected: Purchase acceleration, illusionary goal progress, and customer retention. *Journal of Marketing Research*, 43(1), 39–58.
[5]Drèze, X., & Nunes, J. C. (2011). Recurring goals and learning: The impact of successful reward attainment on purchase behavior. *Journal of Marketing Research*, 48(2), 268–281.
[6]Gjesme, T. (1974). Goal distance in time and its effects on the relations between achievement motives and performance. *Journal of Research in Personality*, 8(2), 161–171.

- *Travel Miles:* Receiving "miles" that can be used toward travel. Each mile represents one dollar spent on the card. And that mile typically carries a monetary value of one penny, or 1% of your *purchases*. (Remember, you're not getting rewarded for payments made to the credit card company or interest accrued. So, the value of the incentive compared to what you have to pay the credit card company is far below 1%.)

And when we cash in on these benefits we view them as being financial windfalls. We view the airline ticket as "free." Or, if we don't have the miles to pay for the whole ticket, we still view the flight as "cheap" when we use miles to *partially* offset its cost.[7]

If you pay off your credit card every month before accruing interest, these incentives represent a nice, albeit *tiny* perk. Every $25,000–$50,000 you spend, you'll get a free domestic plane ticket. Hurray! Go see your mother. It'll make her so happy.

You could even become like "The Points Guy" who has become an Internet celebrity for his ability to get epic amounts of free stuff through credit card rewards.[8] But, again, doing this *requires* paying off your entire balance each and every month before you accrue interest. Otherwise, you're getting yourself into real trouble. And odds are, you're going to get yourself into real trouble.

About 2/3 of credit card holders carry a balance forward every month.[9] This means the allure of credit card incentives is a gateway perk to indentured servitude. The average interest rate for a credit card is approximately 17%.[10] Many cards greatly exceed that rate. As you have seen illustrated elsewhere in this book, that is a profound amount of interest when compounded.

As a refresher, let's look back at the example of a $200,000 mortgage. At 6% on a 30-year mortgage, you're paying $431,676

---

[7]Drèze, X., & Nunes, J. C. (2004). Using combined-currency prices to lower consumers' perceived cost. *Journal of Marketing Research*, 41(1), 59–72.
[8]www.ThePointsGuy.com
[9]Wolff-Mann, E. (2016, February 6). The average American is in credit card debt, no matter the economy. *Money*. https://money.com/average-american-credit-card-debt/. Accessed on October 3, 2022.
[10]Black, M., & Frankel, R. S. (2022, September 2). What is the average credit card interest rate? *Forbes Advisor*. https://www.forbes.com/advisor/credit-cards/average-credit-card-interest-rate/. Accessed on October 3, 2022.

for that $200,000 loan. At 17%? $1,026,486. At 28% (also a realistic rate)? $1,680,416. Dang! So, you can see how a free airline ticket here and there is no skin off the credit card company's nose.

We sign up for rewards cards imagining that we will pay the card off every month and use the miles to go on safari in Kenya. But the truth is, most of us carry balances on our cards and end up paying thousands in interest.

And the rewards? We do NOT end up using them to go on safari in Africa. Instead, we use the miles to fly to Cincinnati to go to the wedding of that guy from the office who – well, we're not quite sure how we made the cut for getting invited. Awkward.[11]

Let's take a look at some offers listed as "best rewards cards" on the credit card marketing website *CreditKarma*.[12] Here we find promotions for two different cards – one for people with good credit and one for those with not-so-good credit.

1. Credit Card 1:
   - Cost: APR of 26.24%, $99 annual fee.
   - Benefit: 1% cash back on eligible purchases.

2. Credit Card 2:
   - Cost: APR of 18.99%–26.99%, annual fee of $95.
   - Benefit/Incentive: Double Miles (approximately 2% of purchases).

Looking at the offers, it should take you back to the chapter on partitioned pricing. As a refresher: the more components to a price, the less likely we are to take all those components into account. Most likely you will remember only one (maybe two, if you're feeling especially "with it" that day) components of the price will become part of our remembered or considered price.

---

[11]Cincinnati is a fun town. I lived there for several years. (Go Bengals!) But it's not the stuff of Hemingway novels.
[12]CreditKarma. (n.d.). Best rewards cards. https://www.creditkarma.com/credit-cards/rewards-cards. Accessed on October 3, 2022.

In the above offers, we have four categories of costs and benefits being presented: introductory APR, regular APR, annual fee, and rewards. And, in looking at those offers, two things should jump out at you:

1. The APR for either cards (18.99%–26.99%) is higher than your average credit card interest rate of 17%.

2. There is an annual fee that will, in all likelihood, negate any benefit you would receive from "rewards."

Annual fees are just a form of partitioned pricing. Of the various costs and benefits likely to receive the consumer's attention, the annual fee is likely to finish a distant third or fourth. You could make the argument that rewards will be the focal point as a significant number of consumers surveyed list it as their first consideration when shopping for credit cards.[13]

For example, the $99 annual fee on the first card will cover incentive costs from $9,900 in purchases. If you pay that balance off over the course of one year, at the stated 26.24% rate of the card, you will have paid $1,462 interest, plus $99 in fees to receive... $99 worth of miles or "cash back."

In other words, you got all hot and bothered about the cash and adventures you were going to have. And really, all you did was pay $1,561 to receive $99 in benefits. But, hey, you're about 40% of the way to getting a "free" flight to Baltimore. Hopefully you'll have enough money for crab cakes after literally paying $4,000 in interest and fees to get the "free" $250 flight.

For every $1 you receive from the credit card company, you're paying *at least* $15 in interest (likely more) to get that benefit. And, yet, any of us will celebrate getting a "free ticket" and feel very smart for having done so.

---

[13]Experian. (n.d.). Survey findings: How to consumers feel about credit cards? https://www.experian.com/blogs/ask-experian/survey-findings-how-do-consumers-feel-about-credit-cards/. Accessed on October 18, 2022.

Not Getting Taken for a [Very Expensive] Ride (or Flight)

So, does this mean that you should never enroll in a credit card incentive program? Probably.

These incentive programs are fine if you pay off your balance every month and are not getting hit with annual fees to be part of the program. And if you're wondering if you might be disciplined enough pay off your card, just look at your past behavior.

Self-awareness is difficult, though. In fact, while researching this book, I found an interview with one of the leading researchers on consumer over-reaction to credit card incentives.[14] This is a person who has painstakingly demonstrated, through many peer-reviewed research papers over an extended period that consumers bury themselves in credit card debt, particularly through these incentives. When asked if he still uses credit cards, he said he did. Why? He "needed the miles".

Do you have a history of paying off your cards? No? Then understand that, save any financial windfall, the likelihood is you're going to continue this pattern regardless of any New Year's resolutions you make.

Maybe you do turn over a new leaf and start carrying a zero balance on your credit card. Fine. Turn over that new leaf on a lower interest card with no annual fee. In the long-term, that will best serve your interests. The truth is, these incentive programs are not dishonest. But they *are* a distraction. It can get you focused on the wrong things. And in the highly complex world of consumer credit, such a distraction can cost you lots of money.

---

[14]Lieber, R. (2014, October 10). The most serious threat when using credit: You. *The New York Times*. https://www.nytimes.com/2014/10/11/your-money/the-slippery-plastic-slope-to-overspending.html. Accessed on July 24, 2024.

13

PLATINUM CARDS

Some will sell their dreams for small desires. Or lose the race to rats.

Get caught in ticking traps. – Neal Peart[1]

Credit card branding is the art of turning precious metals into fool's gold.

In 1966, American Express (Amex) introduced its "Gold" card for higher income customers with elite credit.[2] This card came with higher spending limits and more favorable terms than the regular green Amex card. The gold card was not only a big success, it became a major status symbol. Flashing that gold card at a restaurant in the 1960s or 1970s was an instant flex telling everyone you were of significant means. You might as well have parked a Porsche™ with vanity plates ("SO-RICH") by your table.

Given the iconic success of the gold card in the mid-1980s, Amex introduced its platinum card for an even higher-end audience. These higher-end cards were also quickly cemented into popular culture as status symbols. As a result, people coveted them. Then marketers of every other credit card started putting "platinum," "sapphire," or

---

[1]Song Subdivisions by the band Rush of their 1982 album "Signals" on Mercury Records. (Neal Peart was their drummer and lyricist.)
[2]Tsosie, C. (2016, May 12). How platinum and gold cards lost their shine. *Forbes*. https://www.forbes.com/sites/clairetsosie/2016/05/12/how-platinum-and-gold-credit-cards-lost-their-shine. Accessed on October 20, 2022.

some other luxury branding on their cards, regardless of the card-holder's wealth or credit.

A quick perusal of the credit card shopping site "Card Rates" shows that, of those cards targeted for those "rebuilding" credit, about half carry with them feature some sort of luxury branding – silver, platinum, etc.[3] Clearly, the metallic designations in this case are more about a desired branding than an indication of financial status or credit.

The gold and platinum cards of today are the equivalent of counterfeit Rolexes™ – a signal of status, so long as no one looks too closely or gives it too much thought.

But is this evolution just a harmless tweak to the branding of credit cards? No.

Research has shown that status-branded cards change buyer behavior relative to their unbranded counterparts. One study showed that consumers with platinum-branded cards used them more often, particularly in social-visible situations (e.g., if your friends/family/associates would be able to see you use it).[4] In other words, people had a symbol of status, so they wanted to use it in front of the people whose opinion of them mattered.

Psychologically, why do status-branded credit cards have such an effect on us? Two primary reasons:

1. We have a strong desire for status.

2. Symbols of status make the need for status salient which, in turn, motivates us to demonstrate status.

OUR QUEST FOR STATUS

Why do we care so much about demonstrating status? Would you believe that the desire for platinum cards dates back to cavemen?

Back then, as we were competing for food, shelter, and mates, status was a key determinant of how hard we had to work to get

---

[3]https://www.cardrates.com/advice/credit-cards-for-rebuilding-credit/
[4]Bursztyn, L., Ferman, B., Fiorin, S., Kanz, M., & Rao, G. (2018). Status goods: Experimental evidence from platinum credit cards. *The Quarterly Journal of Economics*, 133(3), 1561–1595.

those things and, as a result, how likely we were to survive.[5] If we lacked status among the other cave people, we had to rely upon, and cooperate with, others a great deal more. It required a lot more work for a lot less return. But, as we acquired status within our group, key resources like food would flow to us more easily from our peers. And when we flirted with that special cave person we've had our eye on? That cave person was more likely to flirt back.

The desire for status is part of our evolution. It is baked into us and remains a significant force in our judgment and decision-making. Now, that desire manifests in things like conspicuous consumption: obvious and intentional acts of consumerism that are visible to others.

People buy Ferraris™ because they are beautiful and fast, yes. But they also buy them because everyone knows they are excruciatingly expensive. Being seen driving one sends a strong and immediate signal to others that you're swimming in money.

The desire for status also manifests in consumption that is not visible to others.[6] High-status behaviors and demonstrations make us feel better. It's a way of reassuring ourselves that we hold a privileged place in society. And this can include not only what we buy but how we buy it.

Think about this. Let's say you kept a spare change jar that, over time, was likely to hold more than $200 in quarters, nickels, and dimes. If you had a date that night and were short on cash, would you just throw that jar in the backseat of your car and use it to pay for everything? Probably not. Admittedly, the logistics of carrying 20 pounds of coins with you everywhere – and spending 10 minutes counting coins every time you wanted to pay for something – are challenging.

Instead, let's say you've rolled all your quarters into $10 bundles so you don't have to count individual coins. Or, perhaps you take your date and jar to a bank or Coinstar™ machine to convert your

---

[5]Murray, G. R., & Schmitz, J. D. (2011). Caveman politics: Evolutionary leadership preferences and physical stature. *Social Science Quarterly*, *92*(5), 1215–1235.
[6]Akerlof, G. A., & Kranton, R. E. (2000). Economics and identity. *The Quarterly Journal of Economics*, *115*(3), 715–753.

coins to bills before going out to dinner. You'd still feel embarrassed. Why?

Shouldn't your date appreciate your ingenuity and resourcefulness? Perhaps. But that's actually beside the point. Maybe your date *does* appreciate that. But *you* feel embarrassed because you're engaging in a low-status action in front of someone who represents a potential mate. You're worried that this person is going to stop flirting back after seeing you pay for a four-star dinner with a three-year harvest of coins from your couch. Paying that way is the act of a person lacking resources or status. And even though you *are* a person lacking resources and status, you don't want to reinforce that point with your date. Instinctually, you feel it might jeopardize things.

HOW SYMBOLS OF STATUS AFFECT US

The psychological effects of platinum and gold card branding are reminiscent of the Oprah Winfrey-hyped self-help book *The Secret*. The book became a national sensation for a period. Even among the many things anointed by The Mighty Oprah (TMO) that became best-sellers, *The Secret*'s success stood out. At the risk of oversimplifying, *The Secret* asserted that the act of visualizing an outcome helps bring that outcome to fruition. The author's specific take was akin to wishing something into existence.

For the record, there *is* research that says visualizing the accomplishment of a goal makes that goal appear more achievable which, in turn, increases motivation and effort.[7] As they say, the lord helps those who helps themselves and the harder you work, the luckier you get. Accomplishments require effort. And effort requires motivation. If you really think something is impossible, it's hard to muster the sustained effort required to achieve a goal. In that sense, visualizing an achievement can help set things in motion.

But the notion that you can achieve a goal by just imagining such an achievement – without putting the work in – is just what it

---

[7]Cheema, A., & Bagchi, R. (2011). The effect of goal visualization on goal pursuit: Implications for consumers and managers. *Journal of Marketing*, 75(2), 109–123.

sounds like: wishful thinking. (My apologies to TMO. Please don't be mad at me or this book. I have kids.) The author of *The Secret* is a prime example. She did not visualize her book into existence. Instead, she had to do the monumental work of conceiving of and writing the book, finding a publisher, and so on.

But there *is* something about the power of suggestion that affects people's behavior. Just thinking about, hearing about, or being in the presence of symbols of certain concepts influences our judgment and decision-making. And this is where *The Secret* and status-branded credit cards are alike. When we surround ourselves with thoughts and images about a topic or concept, it changes our behavior.

In a famous psychology paper, researchers presented images and concepts to people who then started to unconsciously demonstrate the behavior that was described to them.[8] In one experiment, the researchers described the concept of rudeness to participants. Afterward, the participants began to interrupt each other more frequently. In another experiment, images of elderly men were presented and the participants began to move more slowly.

In psychology, this is called "priming." Images and words have the ability to activate concepts in our mind and we, without knowing it, exhibit these concepts for a time. In pop culture we think of this as subliminal messaging where a millisecond message about buying M&Ms™ is snuck into a movie in hopes it will send us running to the concession stand. It's not something obvious or even noticeable. Yet, it can impact our behavior.

Would it then be difficult to believe that if you endow a person with a symbol of wealth like a "Platinum Card," that the person's behavior would change accordingly? Consumers – regardless of means – getting cards branded "platinum" tend to spend more. They adopt spending habits more similar to their high-credit counterparts.

OK, marketers. Good job. You managed to get customers spending more by wanting to imitate the spending habits of people

[8]Bargh, J. A., Chen, M., & Burrows, L. (1996). Automaticity of social behavior: Direct effects of trait construct and stereotype activation on action. *Journal of Personality and Social Psychology, 71*(2), 230.

with significant means. But, the problem is that while any consumer can imitate a high-credit consumer's spending (at least for a time), they can't imitate their ability to pay. Either you have the money or you don't. No mindset is going to change that, at least not in the short-term. And that's a problem if you're the poor schnook stuck paying the bill.

Now, when marketers introduced status-branding for credit cards, did they think they were evil geniuses who were going to manipulate behavior? Probably not. A lot of marketing is like the proverbial lab rat trying to get a tasty pellet. The rat pushes multiple levers until it finds the one that gives a pellet. Then, the rodent keeps clicking that lever until it stops giving pellets.

For marketers, instead of looking for the lever that will give us pellets, we are searching for the combination of product and message that will generate a response from consumers. Once we find that combination, we keep hitting it until we stop getting the response. "People seem to really like the platinum-branded cards more than the other cards. So, let's put out more platinum cards." Pretty simple, really. And fairly innocent – so long as you don't contemplate the ultimate consequences when you're marketing things like debt.

Over time, do credit card marketers notice that gold and platinum card holders – even those with bad credit – spend more than consumers with different cards? Absolutely. It's a marketer's job to notice. In fact, it would be malpractice to not notice or at least ask the question. And if a marketer asks that question, there's mountains of data that give a definitive answer.

Credit card marketers may not know *why* this is happening. Legally, they're not required to care. But when you're targeting low-income consumers with high interest debt in a way that results in them spending more. . . the consequences should be obvious. In theory, it should tug at your conscience. In theory.

THE CURE FOR STATUS-SEEKING

If we're hard-wired to pursue status, does that mean we are mindlessly driven in the direction of any status-related object?

Of course not. When it comes to human psychology and behavior, there are no absolutes, just tendencies. Certain types of people are more susceptible to certain tendencies.

So, who is more susceptible to wanting to obtain and use status-branded credit cards? Those who have a weak sense of self-esteem. Self-esteem is a term we hear thrown about all the time. We have a feel for what it means, but let's look at its explicit meaning. Specifically, researchers define self-esteem as feelings of self-worth and self-liking.[9]

As humans, we have all known feelings of worthlessness at one time or another. Maybe we can point to an event that makes us feel that way. Or maybe we just wake up one day and it is upon us and we can't explain why.

We understand that it's not just a mood. Worthlessness is a state of being that shakes the ground beneath our feet. It alters our decisions and actions, almost always for the worse. A lack of self-esteem makes us indecisive, volatile, and afraid.

As friends, parents, and family members, we want to make sure that the people we love know that they are both loved and loveable. We instinctually understand that this is the most vital nourishment we can give. Building someone's self-esteem gives that person a sense of safety and belonging in the world. Self-esteem puts us on solid, unshakeable ground and gives us the courage to pursue happiness.

STATUS VERSUS SELF-ESTEEM

What do status and self-esteem have in common?

First, they are both feelings. Second, they are highly related, but distinct. Status is an *external* validation of worth, while self-esteem is more internally driven. Status is more volatile and largely derived from your position – real or perceived – relative to others. That position can be financial, social, or political.

---

[9]Rosenberg, M. (1965). Rosenberg self-esteem scale. *Journal of Religion and Health*.

We don't think of status as a feeling. It's something we assume is more measurable or quantifiable – like, if you're rich, you have high-status. While wealth contributes to our feeling of status, it's far from the only consideration.

For example, if you're a billionaire and your boyfriend or girlfriend breaks up with you, you are going to feel low-status despite your extraordinary wealth. Conversely, if you have low income but are president of your favorite community organization or captain of your softball team, you're going to feel high-status despite your limited financial means.

Self-esteem is more internally driven. It is a composite both of how you feel about yourself in the moment as well as how you feel about yourself over the long-term. Some people's personalities are prone to high self-esteem. Others are prone to low. It can also be driven by a person's own sense of his or her abilities and accomplishments.

When people have feelings of low self-esteem, a common tonic for that malady is to pursue status and attempt to boost the feelings of worth that others confer upon you. But that pursuit is a fool's errand – at least in the long-term.

THE DIRTY SECRET ABOUT CONSUMPTION, STATUS, AND SELF-ESTEEM

Why do people with low self-esteem seek status-branded cards? It's a form of positive reinforcement. Does external validation enhance your self-esteem? Yes! Or, at least, in some cases. And for a short period of time.

We're supposed to say money can't buy happiness and materialism is evil. But the truth is, sometimes buying something nice for ourselves *does* make us feel better. And, if you're someone of limited means, that's particularly true.[10] Capitalist economies place a social value on financial success and material goods. To lack wealth and material goods carries a stigma with it. And that stigma often lowers self-esteem.

[10]Li, J., Lu, M., Xia, T., & Guo, Y. (2018). Materialism as compensation for self-esteem among lower-class students. *Personality and Individual Differences*, *131*, 191–196.

Buying something nice for yourself is often an effective, short-term tonic for low self-esteem in those cases. It's not going to change your life forever. But if a person feels they are lacking in a certain area and they are able to compensate for it, such compensation will provide relief from the stresses on your self-esteem. Even if only temporarily.

Of course, the challenge here is for people to live within their means and not bury themselves in debt. Plus, if someone suffers from chronically low self-esteem, buying something every time you're feeling bad about yourself (which, for that person, is most of the time) invites a whole host of other problems.

Studies of compulsive shoppers show low self-esteem to be a key contributing factor to that compulsion, suggesting that these shoppers are more in search of status than stuff.[11] Retail therapy. We've all done it. Though some do it more than others.

But when you add a high-status branding to that therapy with something like a platinum card, it's like a double-hit of the drug of choice for the self-esteem challenged.

SO WHAT CAN WE DO?

The likelihood of getting companies to stop doing things that make them more money is, well, nil. Rather than launch a doomed consumer protection campaign against credit card companies, let us focus on simple steps we can take to resist our Neanderthal impulses as they relate to status-branded credit cards.

First, if status-branded credit cards influence people to spend more... are there certain types of cards that might prime you to spend less? Yes!

Studies have shown that value branding – that is, something branded by a company associated with low prices or saving money – prime people to spend less.[12] Cut up your platinum cards and

---

[11]O'Guinn, T. C., & Faber, R. J. (1989). Compulsive buying: A phenomenological exploration. *Journal of Consumer Research*, 16(2), 147–157.
[12]Laran, J., Dalton, A. N., & Andrade, E. B. (2011). The curious case of behavioral backlash: Why brands produce priming effects and slogans produce reverse priming effects. *Journal of Consumer Research*, 37(6), 999–1014.

settle into the dullest and most thrift-branded cards you can find! Do away with your platinum Louis Vuitton™ branded card and sign up for a plain WalMart™, Dollar General™ or Goodwill™ branded card. And if the card features a tagline like WalMart's "Save more. Live better™," all the better.

Second, if you suffer from low self-esteem and tend toward retail therapy to treat it, engage in simple, non-consumption tasks to raise your feelings of self-worth. Avoid or combat negative self-talk. Engage in positive or encouraging self-talk. Set simple goals you are likely to accomplish. Spend time in situations, or with people, that make you feel good about yourself. Avoid situations and people that don't. Reduce social media consumption – or eliminate it all together.

Over many millennia, evolution has programmed us with a number of drives and behaviors. Some of them, like the drive to cooperate with others and form communities, continue to serve both of us as individuals and a society. Others, like the drive for status, have a more complicated place in the modern world.

There can be positive benefits to pursuing status, like ambition and achievement. However, in modern society, the drive for status often results in behaviors and decisions (like compulsive shopping) that undermine our own safety and security. We may over spend, over consume, sacrifice our principles, and more. To be mindful of our status-driven behaviors, and how to keep negative ones in check, can be vital to our long-term well-being.

SUMMARY TWO

Hello there! You've made it quite a long way through this book. In fact, you are so very close to being done. Congrats! And since we have covered some more ground, it seems time for another recap:

- **There are several forces that shape our evaluation of a price including reference prices – our stored memory of prices for similar goods – and price transparency – the ability to do a search for the prices of competitive offerings.** Additionally, most of the items we buy feature one price, making the value of that good easy to evaluate. Consumer credit products are uniquely difficult to evaluate in terms of price as there are multiple price components, little transparency, and interest rates literally change every day.

- **Compounding interest rates defy human intuition causing many of us to underestimate the true cost of a loan.** As a price that is applied, and constantly reapplied, to a produce, and which might change over time, most of us do not understand the true price.

- **Consumers are given a false sense of security on the prices for financial products.** Being able to compare prices for things (price transparency) gives consumers power to get a better deal. But the complexity of pricing in financial products enables lenders to create the illusion of price transparency. That illusion is based in an upfront price (interest rate) that doesn't capture the total cost.

- **When a product has multiple pricing components, we fail to take all of those components into account.** We typically remember one price for a good. As such, the more pricing elements there are for a good, the less likely we are to understand the total cost.

- **The later a price component is introduced in the buying process, the more likely it is to be tolerated.** The process of "drip pricing" – adding costs to the consumer after they have already committed to buying a good – makes consumers more likely to accept add-on costs, even if it substantially diminishes the value of the initial deal.

- **Consumers over-react to rewards incentives like receiving "airline miles" for credit card purchases, often making more frequent purchases to receive these rewards.** The value of the incentive in miniscule compare to the amount of interest they are likely to pay for these purchases.

- **Research has shown that credit cards with status branding like "Platinum" have spent more, regardless of their ability to afford it.**

14

WHAT SHOULD BE

For all of this talk about what is being done in a harmful way, let's talk about how things *should* be done. After all, we need loans and credit! For goodness sake, the Broadway smash *Hamilton* was about the guy who established a system of credit for the United States.[1] No doubt, the sequel *Salmon!*, about the person who established Treasury bonds (Treasury secretary Salmon Chase) is in the works.

But after all the discussion of our own blind spots in evaluating financial products and the actions of some marketers to exploit them (intentionally or not), we are left with the question of "What we should do about it?" or "How should things work?" The challenge is three-fold.

First, marketers need to be constrained from their natural impulses to make the quickest sale possible. Speed kills... especially when it comes to comprehending something complex. In financial services, that speed is often at the expense of consumers understanding what they're buying. It doesn't mean that the marketing of financial products is inherently dishonest or malicious. It's a marketer's job to move product, after all. But the potential for running rough shod over a consumer is great when the good or service being promoted is:

- Essential.

- Difficult to understand.

---

[1] "Hamilton" by Lin Manuel Miranda, Copyright 2015.

Understanding that a marketer's default setting is to "always be closing," any constraint on these marketing practices must come in the form of rules and regulations.

Second, there are segments of the population who are at an inherent disadvantage when it comes to consumer finance. They lack access to the resources to even have a reasonable chance at financial stability and growth. But there are some simple remedies to this.

Lastly, we as consumers need to position ourselves to avoid common mental mistakes or miscalculations related to debt. In a perfect world, with perfect brains, we could just make great decisions all the time. As this book has detailed at length, and what our experience has told us, is that such perfection does not exist. The good news is that there are simple precautions we can take to enhance our chances of making quality financial decisions.

OUR EXISTING CONSUMER PROTECTION LAWS ARE OBSOLETE

As discussed, figuring out the true cost of a loan is hard. Compounding interest makes your head spin, and then you often have to conduct a scavenger hunt to find all of the components of price related to a loan. Those components are in different places, called different things, and revealed at different times. All of these potential differences in price presentation represent an opportunity for a borrower to be confused or misled.

The *intent* of a law like The Truth In Lending Act (TILA) is to prohibit many of these "tricks" that obscure the true cost of a loan. The *effect* of certain aspects of TILA is to provide cover for bad actors.

Those who crafted TILA so many years ago appeared to have had a firm grasp on the marketing "tricks of the trade" for predatory lenders. But the language of that law – enacted in 1968 – is written for a world long-since passed. While it may have been effective in its time, the law does not anticipate the marketing platforms of today and provides ample "wiggle room" for unscrupulous marketers.

A bad faith lender can take many actions that violate the *spirit* of the law but not the *letter* of the law. When the cost of a loan is presented as a flat fee such as with pay day lenders or check cashing stores, TILA requires lenders to calculate the equivalent annual interest rate and present it "in a clear and conspicuous" way. "Clear and conspicuous" is a loophole through which the lender could drive a Brinks™ truck.

A simple Google query will show you that predatory lenders will provide an APR, but in smaller print and/or on separate web pages from the core offering or cost information. The motivation behind deemphasizing the APR in such a way is clear. It is an attempt to obscure, if not outright hide, information that will give the customer a true sense of the loan's cost. This enables a lender to comply with the letter or law while still executing the slight-of-hand those laws were meant to eliminate.

When you also consider that this law was written 30 years before Internet use became mainstream and 40 years before the iPhone was introduced, it is woefully inadequate. In 1968, the likely form of marketing information was a printed brochure – a small, fixed format. Such a finite format is easy enough to search and comprehend. While the content of that brochure may not be either riveting or clear, most of us can muster the 10 minutes to read it and feel confident we've see the required legal disclosures.

Now, that marketing information is on the Internet – a format that is infinite in its capacity and offers a myriad of opportunities to hide or obscure things on separate pages. Plus, marketers can block search engines from indexing those pages with a simple line of code making it even harder to find.[2] Clearly, a clarification of the old rules – if not an introduction of new rules all together – is needed.

---

[2]Elliott, J. (2019). TurboTax deliberately hid its free file page from search engines. *ProPublica*. https://www.propublica.org/article/turbotax-deliberately-hides-its-free-file-page-from-search-engines. Accessed on September 30, 2024.

BRINGING TILA INTO THE 21ST CENTURY

Taking all of this into account, regulators need to update the lending rules on the books with greater specificity to protect some of consumers' most common psychological vulnerabilities. These include:

1. To avoid manipulation of people's attention and ability to process costs, APRs need to be presented on the same line and with the same size, color, and font as fees. This will facilitate direct comparison and comprehension of the relative costs of the loan.

2. To avoid exploiting escalating commitment of borrowers in loans which take longer to process (like mortgages), a complete estimate of costs needs to be provided at the beginning of the process, and those costs should not be allowed to change. This will avoid putting the borrower in a position of accepting surprise (and potentially unjust) costs out of fear of having to repeat the protracted process with a new lender.
   - Similarly, to avoid upselling to consumers when they are fatigued or stressed (such as with extended warrantees when buying a car), all such product promotions should be presented up front and with the total cost and monthly cost (if rolled into a loan) presented.

In addition to this, there are new financial products and platforms such as peer-to-peer lending, crypto currency, and digital payments that aren't clearly regulated by TILA. Updating TILA would help give consumer protections a much-needed modernization.

PROTECTING VULNERABLE POPULATIONS

A recurring theme in this book is that economically disadvantaged people fall prey to predatory lending the most.

Part of the reason is that people with fewer resources tend to have lower credit ratings which results in higher interest rates. Though financial and economic theory supports charging higher interest rates to "higher risk" borrowers, it does have the effect of making the disadvantaged more likely to stay that way. The lowest rates are enjoyed by the well-heeled while the most expensive rates are placed on those least able to afford them.

Another explanation is that the poorer you are, the less likely you are to have adequate education or experience in finance. Generational poverty perpetuates this. If kids aren't learning finance in school, they're probably also not learning it at home. Guidance and mentorship on financial matters are invaluable and those things are often lacking in an impoverished environment.

But the truth is, there's research to suggest that the effects of financial education fade in the long-term, particularly among the poor.[3] So, what is financially hurting the people who can least afford such harm.

The biggest factor is a lack of options.

One recent study found that the presence of blood banks in impoverished areas – places where people can sell their plasma – decreases the use of high-interest lenders by 13% on average.[4] This suggests disadvantaged people understand the perils of excessive – and excessively expensive – debt. Given the chance to avoid such debt, they do.

The problem is most impoverished areas – whether it's the inner city or remote, rural areas – have nothing *but* predatory lenders. There are no mainstream financial options available to them. And, a lack of such options perpetuates the cycle of poverty when people have to pay too much for the financial services the rest of us use at market rates. Without those options, people can't pay their bills, save money, or start businesses.[5]

Perhaps the economics of placing retail banking locations in poorer neighborhoods doesn't make financial sense to banks. It probably doesn't. And, for better or worse, a free enterprise system means those companies have the right to make that decision.

---

[3]Fernandes, D., Lynch Jr, J. G., & Netemeyer, R. G. (2014). Financial literacy, financial education, and downstream financial behaviors. *Management Science*, 60(8), 1861–1883.
[4]Dooley, J. M., & Gallagher, E. A. (2024). Blood money: Selling plasma to avoid high-interest loans. *The Review of Financial Studies*, 37(9), hhae018.
[5]Faber, J. W. (2019). Segregation and the cost of money: Race, poverty, and the prevalence of alternative financial institutions. *Social Forces*, 98(2), 819–848.

But where private enterprise can't provide due to market dynamics, there is a place for the government to lend a hand. State and federal government offices in these areas can provide a store front for mainstream banking services. For instance, Social Security, Departments of Motor Vehicles, and the US Post Office locations have:

- multiple offices in most every community (particularly those with fewer financial resources);
- financial transactional capabilities;
- the ability to track personal accounts.

In other words, the pieces are already in place at these facilities to provide market rate financial services in areas not currently served by mainstream banks. And if the notion of government provided financial services makes people (or banks!) uncomfortable, these government office "store fronts" could tie to private banks via the internet. The government could provide the retail location, while the banks could manage the money.

Or, as has been demonstrated effectively in other countries, the licensing of new branch locations in more affluent areas can be tied to opening branches in less affluent ones.[6] If a bank wants to open five locations in downtown Manhattan, regulators could require they also open one in rural, upstate New York or an unbanked section of South Bronx.

PUTTING OURSELVES IN A POSITION TO SUCCEED

To know thyself is the beginning of wisdom.
                                                    – Socrates

While we wait for the economic and regulatory environments to get their act together and throw us a bone, we are all stuck with the

---

[6]Burgess, R., & Pande, R. (2004). Can rural banks reduce poverty? Evidence from the Indian social banking experiment. *American Economic Review*, 95(3), 780–795.

difficult work of navigating financial services as they exist today. To do that, we need to figure some ways to reduce the chances of making bone-headed financial decisions. Since our natural state is to underestimate the cost of financial services, this means we have take certain precautions to guard against mistakes we tend to make.

Metaphorically speaking, we stand barefooted in the playroom of life with a floor covered in Legos™ – each representing a common bias, misjudgment, or distraction that leads us astray in financial decision-making. If we can't clear a Lego-free path for ourselves... ouch. We need to help ourselves wherever we can. Any opportunity to enhance our chances of making a better decision should be seized. What follows are some simple steps we can take to enhance our financial health and make better decisions.

PAYROLL DEDUCTIONS/AUTOMATIC SAVING

Remember when we talked about our tendency to easily commit to something in the future, underestimating how hard it is to fulfill such a commitment? Earlier in the book it was in the context of promising weeks in advance to help a friend move or committing to a loan today that will be difficult to pay off in the future. You want to help the friend move, or buy yourself a car, so you commit, underestimating how difficult the move or the payments will be.

But there are scenarios where you can make such a dynamic work to your advantage: saving money. Putting money away every month is difficult. Life is complicated and expensive. But if you opt in to plans that automatically increase your savings rate whenever your pay increases, you can make that tendency work to your advantage.

Research has shown that opting in to automatic saving or payroll deductions increases savings rates.[7] First, commit to automatic saving. Then, commit to automatic increases in saving as your income increases. Those who committed, in advance, to

---

[7]Thaler, R. H., & Benartzi, S. (2004). Save more tomorrow™: Using behavioral economics to increase employee saving. *Journal of political Economy*, 112(S1), S164–S187.

allocate a percentage of future raises to savings were able to save at a much higher rate.

It is evocative of Social Security. That program is sometimes called an "entitlement." Or, perhaps it's thought of as a "hand out." The truth is, it's merely a public pension program designed to decrease poverty among senior citizens. Left to their own devices, people often don't save for retirement. Part of the reason is that the notion of retirement when you're in your 20s is an abstraction. The thought of being old when you're young seems either an impossibility or much further off than it actually is.

The other part is it's just hard to save. There are always surprise expenses and new desires. As a result, people were not saving along the way and found themselves destitute in their later years.

The government decided to create a mandatory pension program with the novel innovation that money would be taken out of a paycheck before it hits an employee's bank account. Sure, from time-to-time, the employee may look at his or her paystub and complain, "Hey! I could have really used that $100!" But, for the most part, the deductions became accepted with an understanding they would provide a future benefit.

Behavioral science would suggest that if social security contributions had to be made manually and/or voluntarily after the money was in the person's account, it would have done one or both of the following:

- Crushed the level of savings for retirement.

- Gotten people in legal trouble for not meeting the mandated level of contributions.

But, with automatic contributions that escalated with the level of income, a higher number of people saved more for retirement. And, it worked! A recent congressional report estimates that Social Security has reduced poverty in seniors by 70%.[8]

---

[8]Congressional Research Service. (2022, December 6). Poverty among the population aged 65 and older.

RE-EDUCATE YOURSELF BEFORE AN IMPORTANT
FINANCIAL DECISION

Just like the French you learned in middle school, the effects of financial education fade over time.[9] You either use it or you lose it. And since no one *likes* educating, let alone *re*-educating, themselves on finance, it puts you at a disadvantage when dealing with a financial services professional who is immersed in finance all day, every day.

If you're not working in finance, your understanding of how credit works and what it costs is neither fresh nor salient at the time you need it. Though you had, at some point, learned these lessons of better financial decision-making and understood the dynamics of things like compounding interest, those lessons will not be there for you – at least not in full force – when you need them. Prior to an important financial decision, it is important to reacquaint your-selves with both the mechanisms of finance *and* the common mis-takes people (e.g., you, me, and everyone else) make.

This does not mean you have to read hundreds of pages of a finance text book prior to making a financial decision. But an article or a podcast or two will help conjure these lessons.

DO THE WORK… EVERY TIME

There is an adage that learning begins at the end of your comfort zone. If you stay immersed in the familiar, you don't actually grow in any meaningful way. While that comfort zone may feel as good as a leather recliner in front of your favorite TV show, not too many important or interesting things are going to happen to you there. You have to get out into the world and experience (and learn) new things that will probably make you uncomfortable at different times.

Financial analysis ranks right up there with cleaning the garage or weight loss in terms of things we like to avoid. For many, just

---

[9]Fernandes, D., Lynch Jr, J. G., & Netemeyer, R. G. (2014). Financial literacy, financial education, and downstream financial behaviors. *Management Science*, 60(8), 1861–1883.

trying to look at numbers in which we are not comfortable in their interpretation is to dive head-first into the deep-end of a pool of anxiety. The second-guessing, the discomfort, and overall frustration of trying to engaging with something we'd rather not makes the job especially difficult. While looking at such information, you may well be thinking, "I just want this to be over." Then, you stop doing the work.

But better financial decision-making comes down to just that – persevering. All of the little psychological pitfalls we've discussed that can lead you astray in finance can be figured out *if* you take the time to do the work. Remember, research has shown the greatest single factor in paying the lowest price possible for a loan is not credit score. It's the amount of time a person spends researching and comparing loans.

The longer a person shops, the more the true cost of a loan becomes apparent. All of those little add-on prices? Over time, you find them and are able to take them into account. Not sure what a loan is supposed to cost?[10] As you do your research, you begin to develop reference prices for that particular loan and a sense of fair value.

But you *cannot* achieve any of those things in your comfort zone. It requires accepting the discomfort that learning brings, asking for help when needed, and having the courage to move forward even when that leather recliner is calling you – loudly.

If you can do that, those little slights of hand that marketers sometimes pull won't seem like magic. They'll be as obvious and hackneyed as noticing a teenage magician tucking the card up his sleeve. You will be able to call out the move and the "magician" or marketer will be embarrassed and retreat.[11]

When that happens, you'll know you're going to be making better financial decisions and paving the way for a better future. And that will be sweet.

---

[10]Most of us aren't.
[11]Simply a metaphor. Do NOT call out a teenage magician! The kid's just learning, after all. Pretend you didn't see it and "ew" and "ah" like the rest of the audience.

www.ingramcontent.com/pod-product-compliance
Lightning Source LLC
Chambersburg PA
CBHW061254220326
41599CB00028B/5654